THE
DYNAMICS
OF
SANCTIFICATION

William E. Hulme

AUGSBURG PUBLISHING HOUSE
Minneapolis, Minnesota

THE DYNAMICS OF SANCTIFICATION

Scripture quotations are from the Revised Standard Version of
the Bible, copyright 1946 and 1952 by the Division of Christian
Education of the National Council of Churches.

Hymns from the *Service Book and Hymnal* (SBH) are used by
permission of the Commission on the Liturgy and Hymnal.

MANUFACTURED IN THE UNITED STATES OF AMERICA

Contents

THE
DYNAMICS
OF
SANCTIFICATION

CHAPTER ONE

The Problem of Sanctification

Any inquiry into the meaning and process of sanctification is fraught with hazards. Even if we were to use a less theological synonym such as holiness, wholeness, spiritual growth, Christian growth, growing in Christlikeness, or saintliness, the problems remain. Sanctification is, as Henry P. Van Deusen has said, "a great and neglected aspect of Christian truth." I believe this neglect is due more to frustration than to disinterest.

Actually, sanctification has been involved in most of the great conflicts within Christendom. Even the great Christological controversies of the fourth century were not unrelated to sanctification. Athanasius, the champion of orthodoxy, defended the full humanity and the full deity of Christ against the Arian heresy. But Athanasius was not concerned only about the person of Christ. He was concerned about what happened to man when he came to know Christ. In fact, it was to defend this point that he fought so valiantly for the deity of Christ. But this has been largely forgotten. Athanasius' point was that God comes to us through Jesus Christ to restore us to an even

I. Source of Conflicts

1

more glorious divine image than that from which we had fallen. It is the image of Christ that we reflect, as a mirror reflects the image of one who stands before it. So it is only as Christ is God in all his fullness that we can be restored to the divine image through knowing him.

The conflict of the Reformation also involved sanctification. M. L. Cozens, a Roman Catholic, says, "The Church teaches that God for Christ's sake *imparts* holiness: Luther taught that God for Christ's sake *imputes* holiness to the sinner."[1] Anglo-Catholic E. L. Mascall also accuses Protestantism of neglecting sanctification. "Why," he asks, "has Protestantism so firmly repudiated the notion that human nature is really transformed by grace and has limited that action of grace to a purely imputed righteousness that leaves human nature essentially unchanged?" Noting the saintliness of certain Protestants, he concludes that the real problem is in Protestant theology. "One of the most striking characteristics of Protestantism when one meets it in its undiluted traditional forms is the violent contrast between its theology and its religion."[2] In other words, when he gets to know the Protestant, he is impressed by his Christian spirit in spite of his Protestant theology.

From the Protestant side, the conflict also relates to sanctification. Luther's disillusionment with the medieval claims of the higher morality intensified his search for a more genuine holiness. Catholic emphasis on the faithful observance of ecclesiastical procedures is to many Protestants a pseudo sanctification. In *A Quest for Holiness*, Adolf Köberle, a Lutheran theologian, perceives in Catholicism a tendency to combine sanctification with justification—a "mingling" which he calls "confused promiscuity." *Justification by faith* is the Reformation's corrective to this *mingling*.

Among Protestants themselves sanctification has continued to be a source of conflict. Because orthodox Protestantism has emphasized justification, Protestantism's left wing has felt that sanctification has been neglected. Pietist, holiness, and social action groups are often a protest against a dead orthodoxy. Although it is far from their intentions, the very concern of these groups for sanctification predisposes them to a Roman Catholic conception of sanctification and justification. While orthodox Protestantism has emphasized the theology of God's redemptive act, the left wing has emphasized the effect of this redemption upon the believer. Rather than what Christ has done for us, they stress what he has done *in* us or what we should do for him.

John Wesley tried to preserve this distinction between sanctification and justification by making justification the first act of grace, and sanctification the second. Today the holiness groups continue this teaching. After the conversion experience the believer awaits with anticipation the second experience, through which he becomes entirely sanctified. There are, of course, varying descriptions of what sinlessness entails. Yet the difference remains. Although salvation belongs to all converts, the elite among the fellowship have been sanctified as well.

These conflicts within Protestantism over sanctification stem in part from the historical situation of the Reformation. Agitated by the polemics of his day, Luther hammered hard on the theme of justification. To some he seemed to minimize sanctification as well as obedience to law. Yet Luther *had* a theology of sanctification. Kierkegaard called it the minor principle in Lutheranism—namely, the necessity of works of love—and insisted that for the sake of the major principle, justification by faith, closer attention had to be paid to the minor principle. In our day Regin Prenter in his book *Spiritus Creator* presents Luther's theology of the cross as his doctrine of sanctification, according to which those who are justified are sanctified by being put to death with Christ and raised again —not once, but again and again.

In contrast to Luther, Calvin emphasized sanctification. In fact, his concern for the good life exposed him to criticism. For Calvin, sanctification centered in the striving of the will to follow the laws of God. He stressed self-discipline, particularly of sensual desires, for the achievement of righteousness. His exhortations to strive and to subdue prepared the way for a legalism that has at times characterized the Calvinist movement. Because Calvin was suspected of being a legalist by his opponents and Luther was accused of neglecting the law (antinomianism), the problem of sanctification continued as a live issue among the bodies of Protestantism. Yet Luther fought against the antinomians of his day, and Calvin wrote one of the clearest definitions of the Christian's freedom from the law in his *Institutes*.

**II.
Current
Complications**

While the historical problems regarding sanctification are still with us, we are disturbed also by current complications of these problems. Ours is an administrative age. Denominational headquarters are staffed with divisional and departmental executives, deputies, associates, and assistants. Each executive is obligated to plan a program. After appropriate surveys and studies, he maps a program that will supposedly achieve results. Naturally these results must be tangible to be perceived. Since results in the area of the Spirit are more often intangible than tangible, this concentration on the tangible can easily distort the meaning of sanctification.

As an example, a certain denomination has produced a program for the promotion of spiritual growth. Its goals and purposes are obviously excellent. But the difficulty arises over how to measure this spiritual growth. To solve this difficulty the denomination devised a self-rating questionnaire concerning such activities as faithfulness in daily prayer, Bible reading, church attendance, Communion attendance, church work, and proportionate giving. In spite of intentions to the contrary, what resulted—what *had* to result—was the creation of a Protestant set of ecclesiastically approved works whereby the more sanctified could be recognized. Phariseeism, ironically, is primarily concerned with maintaining the good and accepted religious customs.

From a practical point of view there are some advantages in having a congregation of Pharisees. What clergyman would not rejoice to have a church in which all of the members attended services regularly, gave proportionately of their income, conducted family devotions, worked hard on the boards and committees of the church, and abstained from all participation in profanity, adultery, and intoxication. He might easily look upon such unanimity as the assurance that he is a good pastor—or at least a successful pastor. The fact that despite all of these fine habits such people may be as far removed from the Spirit of Christ as the original Pharisees is uneasily ignored. They *look* good, and in our administrative age we may too quickly settle for this.

Even as it may take an American to see the weaknesses in the churches of Europe, so it may take a European to see our weaknesses. We need to listen to Karl Barth when he warns, "What we might possess would certainly not be our redemption. It would have to be something visible, tangible, whether outwardly or inwardly. But whatever is palpable, visible, is temporal and subject to the inescapable dialectic of everything that belongs to the temporal order."[3] Dietrich Bonhoeffer is equally clear. "What matters in the Church is not religion but the form of Christ, and its taking form amidst a band of men. If we allow ourselves to lose sight of this, even for an instant, we inevitably relapse into that programme-planning for the ethical or religious shaping of the world."[4]

Today we are preoccupied with mental health. The psychiatrist has been called the arch-priest of society and psychiatry described as the "queen of the sciences." We have developed a religious psychiatry in which the insights of Freud have been utilized in the propagation of the Christian message. Under the initiative of the clergy, minister and psychiatrist are becoming increasingly cooperative—to the benefit of patients. Although rewarded by this rapprochement, the ministry has also been put on the defensive. The inferiority that pastors often experience in the presence of other professional people has not been helped by his association with the psychiatrists. While it is commonplace for a physician to address a group of pastors, it is highly unusual for a pastor to address a group of physicians. Although it is very profitable to pastors to listen to those of the other helping professions, it is questionable whether the pastor should look to the psychiatrist as an authority in pastoral care. The implication of such authority would be that the goals of pastor and physician are essentially the same, and they are not. So the pressure remains upon the clergy to justify religion to the psychiatrist by identifying the peace that passes understanding with mental health, the salvation of the soul with emotional stability, and the forgiveness of sins with the overcoming of neurotic symptoms.

In such an atmosphere we should expect that sanctification would be understood primarily in terms of emotional health. Although there is nothing unchristian about emotional health, the question is whether it is tantamount to sanctification—or even a necessary concomitant of sanctification. Regardless of what answer we give to this question, we find it difficult in our day to recognize any saint apart from these qualities of emotional health.

Ours is a day of stress upon social rather than personal ethics. The social upheaval that is characterizing our world is experienced also in our own country. Previously it was the rise of the labor movement and now it is the rise of the Negro. All over the world the underprivileged are demanding social and economic equality. Naturally these social problems have been a challenge to the church. Much of the former emphasis upon sanctification among Methodists and Congregationalists has been channeled into these social concerns. These current issues have helped to meet our desperate need for a cause. Communism appeals to those who would build a new economic and social utopia here on earth—offering a challenge to those seeking new frontiers. Our western democratic ideals are apparently losing their power to provide this challenge except under the distorted forms of anticommunist fanaticism. But picket lines, freedom riders, sit-ins, freedom marchers, and strikes against nuclear testing seem to be restoring life to these ideals. At least these are all distinctly free-world occupations, which would indicate that the atmosphere of democracy is still a favorable atmosphere for a creative challenge.

Although the social ethics emphasis counteracts individualistic tendencies in sanctification, it raises disturbing questions in the area of motivation. Is the *cause* serving our needs more than we the *cause?* Also, one's social action may actually become his religion rather than the expression of it. The crusader for a cause may simply be projecting his own dissatisfaction with himself upon society. The fact that he is more often negative in his activity than positive exposes him to this possibility. At the same time the prophets of Israel could also be accused of being negative. In our analytically-minded age it is wise to be cautious with our analytical conclusions. Suffice it to say that attacking social evils is a Christian vocation; yet it is no more identical with sanctification than any other good work.

III.
Problems
in
Presentation

Sanctification presents a problem even in the method of its presentation. The usual media are those of systematic theology, mystical contemplation, or ethics. Systematic theology has the advantage of bringing order and coherence to this normally chaotic area. But the difficulty is that such order and coherence may stem more from the mind of the systematician than from the actual process of sanctification. Systematic theology produces the descriptive map, rationally and intellectually oriented; it is the catechetical procedure, aimed at getting our thinking straight. Sanctification, on the other hand, is illusive and personal. Between the systematic map of the sanctification process and the actual process itself there remains a great gulf. The description may seem rather academic and abstract to one who is attempting to use it for his own development in sanctification. The system that looks good on paper may not be so good in effecting a transfer to actual life experience. In fact the presentation itself is similarly limited. Köberle's *A Quest for Holiness* is an example in point. Although he allows himself to relate his map of sanctification in one instance to the experiences of Paul and Luther, Köberle admits that "it might appear a questionable procedure" in "a systematic presentation." He goes on to say that his purpose in this irregularity is actually to illustrate the crisis of legalism rather than any positive experience in Christian growth.[5]

Most of the more popular treatises in the area of sanctification have been presented in the medium of mystical contemplation or pietistic devotion. Though differing in emphasis, mysticism and pietism are united in their concentration upon the believer's personal relationship with the immanent God. Both are experience-centered. With their emphasis upon the emotion of joy and the serenity of spirit, the pietistic and mystical schools are the religious predecessors of our current mental health movement. Mysticism has its dark night of the soul; yet the primary mood is ineffable joy in the presence of the Immanent One. The published papers of the Keswick Conventions in England, begun in 1875 and held annually for the specific purpose of "promoting practical holiness," illustrate this priority of enjoyment also in pietistic devotion. The goal of the movement is always the blessedness of the "Spirited-filled life."[6] In America the growing movement known as Yokefellow Associates is retreat-centered like Keswick, but is distinctly American in its utilization of group dynamics and in its cultivation of emotional health.

The shortcomings in this medium of presentation are opposite from those of systematic theology. Highly personal and feeling-centered, mysticism and pietism may only widen the gulf with the reader whose emotional development does not coincide with this type of expression. There is also a problem in the method itself. To map the way to sanctification in specific activities and exercises may lead to a caricature of sanctification rather than to sanctification. Also the very demand for progress implied in the pursuit of holiness makes it difficult for one to continue to face the plaguing contrasts within his own soul.

The medium of ethics, like systematic theology, is academic and rational. In fact, it is simply the other side of systematic theology. In ethics we focus upon the conduct of the sanctified rather than the sanctification process that leads to the conduct. Ethics is concerned with the decisions that a Christian must make in our complex society, decisions that are often between two goods or two evils rather than between good and evil. Although the patterns of systematic theology are present in the medium of ethics, as for example in a book like *Christian Ethics* by Paul Ramsey, they are present only as background to illustrate the nature of the decisions confronting the Christian as he interacts with his environment. In current presentations of theological ethics, the existential moment and one's encounter with the will of God rather than obedience to a systematic code of conduct have become the basis for ethical decision. We find this emphasis in Bonhoeffer's *Ethics* and a theological basis for it in Barth who writes "[God] wants man to be His creature, His partner, and His child. What this means for each of us here and there, today and tomorrow, is decided by the free word of the free Lord in ever-renewed encounter between God and an individual."[7] An older source for this position is *Fear and Trembling*, in which Kierkegaard examines the decision of Abraham to offer up his son Isaac. Kierkegaard's fascination for this decision grew out of his own dedication to the premise that whatever the believer perceives as the will of God for him in the present moment must take precedence over all other considerations, including those of reason and desire. But the dynamics involved in this intuitive realization of the ultimate obedience remains for the most part outside of his concern. The shortcomings of ethics as a medium for the presentation of sanctification coincide with the limitation of ethics to the actual decisions of the sanctified, Although these decisions are an important part of the meaning of sanctification, they remain only a part.

In contrast to these usual media I have selected *pastoral* theology as the frame of reference for a discussion of sanctification. Since spiritual growth has always been allotted to the shepherding aspect of the ministry, the theological discipline governing this shepherding activity could logically be the medium for the study of spiritual growth. This medium may also manifest weakness in the course of our study—which weaknesses we shall attempt to recognize. From our beginning vantage point, however, pastoral theology possesses the virtue of uniting the other three media. As the middle ground between systematic theology and ethics, it takes systematic theology to its ethical consequences. In its concentration upon theology's relationship to the inner life, it also takes systematic theology to its origin in the divine-human encounter. On the other hand, by its involvement with human problems, pastoral theology takes the experience of man with God to its consequent ethical decisions. It may also trace these ethical decisions to the experience with God out of which they come.

The advent of clinical pastoral education has further equipped pastoral theology as a medium for a theological inquiry into sanctification. In this supervised ministry to persons in need (normally within the controls of an institution such as a hospital), one's understanding of the Word of God is deepened. The clinical approach is preceded and followed by theological reflection. In its clinical orientation pastoral theology maintains that necessary tension between reflection and experimentation. Focusing upon the personal relationship between God and man and between man and man, pastoral theology encompasses both the comprehension of the systematician and the mystery of the mystic, thus occupying the middle ground between scientific analysis and poetic perception.

By uniting the revelation of God with the dynamics of human behavior, pastoral theology is the strategic motif within which to explore the subtleties of sanctification.

The pastoral care which grows out of pastoral theology is the shepherding aspect of the ministry which relates itself directly to the crises in life which characterize the way of growth. At the same time this shepherding ministry is related directly to the Word of God. This mutuality in pastoral theology between the Word of God and the lives of people makes it a middle axiom in the theological disciplines oriented both in its deposit of truth and in its functional expression as a frame of reference in which to study sanctification.

IV.
Truth
or
Coherence

Each experience in the Christian pilgrimage provides a fresh insight into the Word of God. This is the kind of learning process that characterizes sanctification. Our inquiry into sanctification will follow this same sequence of inpressions. In following this procedure we are risking a possible loss of unity and integration. On the other hand, if we insist upon unity and integration, we may suffer an even greater loss. It is precisely this need for coherence that has continually corrupted our understanding of sanctification. Accepting this limitation is itself an insight into sanctification.

Historical Christianity has its chronological sequence. Christ was born, conducted his ministry, was crucified, dead and buried, and raised again from the dead. The believer's pilgrimage in sanctification is also historical, but the sequence is missing. The division of cause from effect is obscured by the simultaneity of the dynamics involved. There can be no sequential theology of an experience in which one is *simul iustis et peccator*—simultaneously justified and a sinner. We can speak about the dynamics of dying to sin, of involvement in creation, and of dependence upon God—as we shall—but the division between what precedes and what follows among these factors is interchangeable. Neither sequence nor coherence is the indigenous quality of the Christian message. Rather we are confronted by the act of God on the human scene. It is our purpose to inquire into what this act has meant and continues to mean in human experience.

Footnotes

1. M. L. Cozens, *A Handbook of Heresies* (London: Sheed & Ward, 1946), p. 72.
2. E. M. Mascall, *The Importance of Being Human* (London: Oxford University Press, 1959), p. 68.
3. Karl Barth, *The Holy Ghost and the Christian Life* (London: Frederick Muller, Ltd., 1938), p. 78.
4. Dietrich Bonhoeffer, *Ethics* (New York: Macmillan, 1955), p. 21.
5. Adolf Köberle, *The Quest for Holiness* (Minneapolis: Augsburg Publishing House, 1938), p. 27.
6. See for example: Stephen Barabas, *So Great Salvation: The History and Message of the Keswick Convention* (London: Marshall, Morgan and Scott, Ltd., 1952) in which the following quotation sums up the Keswick emphasis: "Sanctification is never a state; it is always an experience—an experience that is the fruit of abiding in Christ. It is not a state, but a maintained condition of purity—a condition of life maintained through living fellowship with Christ."
7. Karl Barth, *The Humanity of God* (Richmond: John Knox Press, 1960), p. 84. See also Stephen Neill, *Christian Holiness* (New York: Harper and Row, 1960), p. 94.

CHAPTER TWO

Sin —Weakness or Defiance

Christian growth is not only growth *toward* something but growth *away* from something. Even as the Christian grows into the fullness of the stature of Christ, so he grows away from the domination of sin. Sin is a word that is used too much by one generation and ignored by another, but in either case the human activity described by this word goes on much the same. How shall we define sin? Since it involves a moral dimension, it is a distinctly human potentiality. The description of the Fall in Genesis obviously sees sin as the rebellion of man against God; as such it has a religious as well as a moral dimension. It is not simply contrary to the will of God; it is a usurpation of the place of God in human life. "You will be like God, knowing good and evil" (Gen. 3:5).

From the perspective of sanctification we are more interested in how a person happens to sin than in any abstract definition of sin. From this point of view it is important for us to know whether we fall into sin because of weakness or defiance—whether it is a matter of human limitation or demonic rebellion. This question confronts

14

us with the paradoxical nature of original sin. Regardless of how many predisposing factors are at work—original and otherwise—the question still remains, do we participate in sin by an act of our will or is our will overcome by the limitations of human existence? The answer to this question is fundamental in any approach to the overcoming of sin.

Thomas Aquinas taught that before one can be guilty of sinning, he must have freedom in which to act and intelligence through which to recognize the realities of the situation. In other words, a person would have to be aware of a choice and have the freedom to make that choice. On the basis of this supposition, the scholastics worked out their clearly defined degrees of sin and rational categories of accountability. The approach seems reasonable. A lack of freedom implies an overpowering predestination from one source or another. A lack of intelligence implies a lack of any conscious awareness. Unfortunately, the scholastics, like most rationalists, overlooked the complexity of human nature and failed to recognize reason's rationalizing capacities. The advent of our personality sciences has necessitated modern attempts to add the dimension of depth psychology to Thomistic principles.

I. Freedom in Sin

We cannot determine a person's freedom or his conscious awareness on the basis of any one moment or one activity in itself. Decisions that an individual has made in the past may lead to a loss of freedom in the present, even as these decisions of the past may lead to a loss of his conscious awareness in the present. Also, succumbing to temptation is often by way of self-deception. The original temptation story is an evidence of this. By raising doubts about her reasons for not eating the forbidden fruit and by giving her plenty of reasons why she should eat it, the tempter succeeded in getting Eve to limit her thinking to what would be gained and to push to the side the warning of what would be lost. However, he could do this only because she wanted to eat the fruit. This juggling of the facts is needed to bring about the necessary anesthetizing of our conscience, so that the desired activity over which we have conflicts may appear more innocent. We shift our focus to reduce our awareness so that we avoid the judgment of conscience, but behind the deception there is the will to deceive and to be deceived.

On the basis of what has been said, we are led to the hypothesis that all sin is essentially intentional. The fact that human beings cannot always fulfill their good intentions was an enigma to Saint Augustine. What lay behind this impotence? To Augustine it was a monstrous or mysterious thing that the mind can give the body directions and the body obeys, but the same mind can give itself directions and nothing happens.

> The mind commandeth the body, and immediately it is obeyed; the mind commandeth itself and it is resisted. The mind commandeth the hand to move, and it is done so promptly that the order given is hardly discerned from the execution. Yet the mind is mind, and the hand is but a part of the body. The mind commandeth the mind to do this or that, it is one and the same, and yet the thing is not done. Whence comes this monstrous thing, and why is it so?[1]

Behind the apparent impotence of the will there is the reality of another and opposing will. What appears as an infirmity of mind is actually a duplicity of mind. This is Augustine's answer to all attempts to account for sin in terms of weakness, imperfection, or error in judgment.

> The mind, I say, commands itself to will a thing, which it would not command, except it would have it to

be done; and yet that which is commanded is not done. But the truth is that it doth not will entirely, and therefore it doth not command absolutely. For it commandeth but so far only as it willeth, and that which is commanded is executed only so far as the thing itself is willed. For the will commands that there should be a will, and not another will but itself. Clearly then the will doth not command fully, and for this cause that which is commanded is not done. For if the willing were full and perfect, it would command that the thing should be done, because it would be done already by the very act of willing. It is therefore no monstrous thing to will a thing in part and not to will it in part, but a plain infirmity of mind; because, being overladen by evil custom, the mind cannot rise wholly even though it be supported by truth. Therefore in such a mind there are two wills, neither of which is entire or perfect; and that which one of them hath, the other wanteth.[2]

Kierkegaard puts it in even stronger terms. Sin is a position, not a negation. By this he means that sin is a manifestation of strength and not of weakness, of decision rather than indecision. So much is sin a position rather than a negation that it is beyond the ability of the sinner to comprehend sin. If he could comprehend it he would be above it. But if it is a position he cannot be above it, rather he is *in* it.

The fact that it is comprehended means precisely that it is negated . . . that is to say that after all it is a position only up to a certain degree, not any more so than that one can after all comprehend it.[3]

Even the sin of omission is a positive affirmation. Rather than being a matter of oversight or weakness it is a matter of resistance. It is the same defiance at work as in the sin of commission. It is the "flesh" in its opposition to the overtures of God. Man's predicament is not only the result of his finitude, that is, his weakness and limitations, but the result also of his freedom, his will to do evil. And it is only as we affirm the latter that we preserve the self from being dissolved in external causalities.

The intentionality of sin is substantiated by clinical observation. The truth of Augustine's two wills comes to light in the dynamics of pastoral care. Significantly the clinical label for this insight is ambivalence, which means literally two wills together. Ambivalence is behind many of our failures and supposed weaknesses. Because the dialogue of pastoral counseling offers unusual insight into the role of this ambivalence, we shall use an excerpt from such a dialogue to illustrate how the opposing wills of a person become separated as he deceives himself in an attempt to satisfy both. The counselee in this instance is a young lady who seemed predisposed to get into trouble sexually. We break into the dialogue as she is saying:

Girl: I really don't want to get into trouble. It's the fellows I date. Once you get a reputation, fellows date you for only one reason.

Pastor: They persuade you against your will.

Girl: Yes—at least this is what I think—or would like to think.

Pastor: You mean you have some doubts here?

Girl: As I told you, I want to be good—to obey God. But I don't know. Something came up the other night that I suppose I should tell you about. It was when I was out again with Mac. I had told myself that I wasn't going to let him take advantage of me again. To my surprise he didn't try.

Pastor: Oh—was this what you noticed?

Girl: Well—no, not all of it. I realized that something was wrong with me. I wasn't particularly satisfied—happy with the situation. I found myself making advances to him. Oh, I hate to

Girl: admit this, but it looks like I want what I don't want, if you know what I mean.

Pastor: You seem to have two selves—and the one you have kept hidden until now.

Girl: I've been trying to figure out why I should be this way—why I should want to tempt someone.

Pastor: I think you are on the right track—it is very important that you see into why you do this.

Girl: Yes, and I've been trying to figure out why. I think it's because I get a certain sense of importance or even power, if a boy makes love to me.

Pastor: On the one hand you want to do what is right and on the other hand you don't want to—because it flatters you—makes you feel you can control people—if you succeed.

Girl: It's frightening. What kind of person am I?

Pastor: It hurts to see yourself as you really are.

II. Weak Flesh

But can all resistance to the Spirit of God be accounted for by human willfulness? Is there not such a thing as being in subjection to natural human limitations? Jesus seems to have thought so when he warned his disciples about the trials that were about to come upon them. "The spirit indeed is willing, but the flesh is weak" (Matt. 26: 41). Here flesh is identified with weakness rather than intentionality and is considered as a hindrance to intentionality. It constitutes our natural faculties for carrying out our spirit's intentions, and the weakness of the flesh is in its subjection to the natural order of sensory and temporal existence. The spirit in this instance is the self as this self seeks to be free from its *bondage* to the stimuli of sense. (This is something other than seeking *freedom* from the stimuli of sense.) It is the spirit of man that differentiates him from the instinctual existence of animal life. The problem in our desire for emancipation from animal existence is that in sharing this existence we are dependent upon sensory experience. The common experiences of fatigue, illness, pain, and hunger which we share with the animal world can be formidable obstacles in carrying out the spirit's intentions. Also the lack of any physical demonstration of affection and other tangible evidences of love can create an emotional handicap that may predispose one to slavery to sexual passion in spite of his desire to maintain sexual discipline.

There were just such circumstances as these behind Jesus' warning to his disciples. We have no reason to doubt the disciples' sincerity when they said they desired to remain loyal to him. This was the intention of their spirits. But Jesus knew that this desire would meet severe resistance from the pressure that would be placed upon their "flesh." At the moment of his arrest there was the sudden and overwhelming threat to their own survival. Their response was fear—fear of what would happen to *them* as separate entities in a material, spatial, temporal, and sensory world. The fear of death is an expression of our transcendence over animal life; it is also a temptation to sin. The instinctual response to such stimuli is self-protection—in this instance, to run from the danger.

Persecutors of all ages have been devious in their application of physical and mental tortures to prevent the intentions of the human spirit from being carried out. None have been more scientifically devious in this respect than our present-day Communists. So successful are their brainwashing tactics that as a prisoner in the Korean war our own General Dean was at the point of committing suicide as the only way of preserving his freedom. Is "entering into temptation" under such circumstances sin? Certainly not in the sense of rebellion against God as one normally understands rebellion in terms of defiance—something born out of hatred for God or even of egotism. Nor need there be any self-deception. There is simply a submission to what is experienced as an overwhelming force from without.

The question of responsibility for defection under duress was a difficult problem of the early church in its periodic reprieves from persecution. How should defection from the faith in the face of torture be interpreted? Significantly the question was not over whether the defection was sin or not, but whether it was forgivable or not. In each instance the church decided that defectors could be readmitted to the church through public confession and repentance. But it was not an easy decision to make and the Donatist and later the Novatian schisms demonstrated the high cost of making it. Yet the fact that it was made reveals that defection under duress was viewed by the church as only the extreme of the normal situation. There are always extenuating circumstances— weak flesh—accompanying expressions of sin—defiant flesh. Even Eve had the serpent to contend with.

Although the human spirit at times has frightfully little potential for carrying out its intentions, we cannot overlook the fact that the predisposing factors contributing to "weak flesh" were not always beyond the spirit's responsibility. When Jesus said, "Watch and pray that you may not enter into temptation" (Matt. 26:41), he was implying that "entering into temptation" was not a foregone conclusion. To *watch* suggests an attitude of preparedness so as not to be caught off guard. To *pray* is to maintain a contact with the Holy Spirit who fortifies our human spirit. Instead of watching and praying, the disciples slept. Again there was the physical overpowering—the fatigue that overcomes one at the close of a full day. But there was also a failure on the part of the disciples to heed the warning. They did not take the warning seriously because

III.
Predisposing
Factors

they did not take their vulnerability seriously. Theirs was the carelessness of an illusory self-sufficiency. There was no overpowering sleepiness when they perceived the danger in its actuality. Their failure to watch-and-pray at this stage of their experience was obviously a predisposing factor to their entering-into-temptation at the later stage.

There is no such thing as a *tabula rasa* for each day. Each of us has his individual hypersensitivities to certain stimuli—hypersensitivities that have developed through the interaction of constitutional and environmental influences. Some of these stimuli are the equivalent of red flags that generate rage within us. Others are black flags that cause us to faint with fear. Still others are white flags that stimulate elation. What we are influences what we do. On the other hand, what we do influences what we are. Any life situation is extremely complicated. One cannot interpret it topologically as he would a picture of a landscape. Rather it is a motion of becoming in which the individual participates as a recipient and as a contributor. Since we are creatures and creators of our weak flesh, the *essence* of sin is not in flesh as weakness but in flesh as defiance. Even those who are defiant toward God are often able to conquer the weakness of the flesh in carrying out their defiant intentions.

**IV.
Ever-Present
Defiance**

Because of these conclusions regarding the nature of sin, we shall concentrate on sin not only as defiance but as *ever-present* defiance of God—the flesh that *lusteth* against the Spirit (Gal. 5:17 KJV). Luther called this essence of sin, concupiscence. Although the word comes from the verb which means simply to desire, it has become associated with sexual desire. Luther's understanding of concupiscence, however, is not primarily sexual desire. It is the corruption of the entire person in egotism, self-seeking, and rebellion against God. We are sinners in all our works. Ecclesiastes says, "There is not a righteous man on earth who does good and never sins" (Eccl. 7:20). Luther interprets this to mean, "There is no man who sins not when he does good."[4] In other words, egotism is involved to some degree, no matter how small, in every human good deed. Reinhold Niebuhr makes this same point to our generation when he says, "The final enigma of history is not how the righteous will gain victory over the unrighteous, but how the evil in every good and the unrighteousness of the righteous is to be overcome."[5]

This is a dynamic concept of sin in contrast to the topological categories of the scholastics against which Luther was reacting. In the words of Luther's English interpreter, Gordon Rupp, "Luther's profound intuitions of the infinite subtleties of human egoism and the dark ferment always at work in the hidden depths of the human soul, anticipate truths which modern psychological science has analytically established."[6] Luther realized that the only way to be free of sin was to have in his heart that pure love of God which the commandment required of him. The scholastics were sensitive to this demand also, but they tried to bring it within reason by saying that this love need not be manifested all the time—that it was sufficient if it occurred from time to time. For Luther this was a compromise of God's law. He took God too seriously for this. Not to take God seriously is defiance, for it makes a fool out of God.[7]

Human egotism is a defiance patterned after Satan's defiance. Sin is not a degeneration to the level of the animal but a deviation in the direction of the diabolical. When we understand his distinctly spiritual conception of concupiscence we can appreciate Luther's predominant emphasis on the First Commandment. "You shall have no other gods," confronts us with the awful question whether we any more than Satan can let God be God. It is the epitome of the entire Law and involves also the Gospel. When God—even the God of love—calls, the flesh throws itself into resistance. In fact, it is the overture of God that activates this resistance.

Because it deals directly with the essence of sin, the First Commandment prohibits this arrogant defiance of divinity and its mitigated counterpart, idolatry. In making a particular into a universal, idolatry is essentially a projection of egocentricity to other finite concerns. While it lacks the appearance of egotism, its ultimate effect is similar. Egotism leads to personal disunity. The collapse of our idol affects us in a way similar to the collapse of our egocentric defense system. No human being can take the role of God. Sooner or later we come to this realization and enter into the crisis of despair. Yet even in despair defiance continues, only now it is a defiance of consolation and hope. As Kierkegaard has pointed out, to refuse to believe in the forgiveness of sin is not only the greater despair, it is the greater sin. So defiance continues even in the collapse of defiance until defiance spends itself in absolute fatigue. It is then that God can be God.

Among the religiously minded, egotism often becomes spiritualized by attaching itself to a religious cause. When it does, it becomes the most elusive saboteur of sanctification. Such egotism is often the unhappy outcome of religious experience. The recipient becomes too elated by the abundance of revelations, not being blessed with sufficient thorns in the flesh. The sense of being called of God is hard to distinguish at times from a kind of megalomania. How easily religion can be used by the ego to fulfill the ego image of being important—of being the man of the hour destined by providence to do something above the ordinary! It is a form of prestige idolatry.

This spiritualizing of egotism is the predominant sin of the professional religionist. Like the builders of the tower of Babel in the Old Testament, the professional religionist builds his towers into heaven, but also like those ancient builders, he is seeking to create a name for himself through his monument. It is difficult to be religious when our profession is religion. Students in pastoral counseling may be able to relate naturally to their counselees in almost every subject except religion. When religion enters the dialogue the student tends to tense up and pontificate. He is no longer responding to the feelings of his counselee, but is rather reacting defensively in an area with which he is personally identified. The subject of God is tied up with his own status, role, and professional security. When religion is used in this way, it becomes religion without the Word of God, for the Word of God demands that the self-centered self must die.

Spiritualized egotism presumes the license to function in the Deity's role of judge. The presumption of judging is an act of arrogance—a manifestation of defiance. Beneath its religious appearance there is the same refusal to let God be God. Our presumption to be the judge of others is also naive because it presumes to locate the seat of evil outside of oneself. This means that the judge's own guard is "down," making him an easy prey to temptation. Unfortunately this critical attitude toward others on the part of "spiritual" people is often taken as a mark of soundness and strength.

V. Pretense of Obedience

Sin at its worst is not only ever-operative defiance but ever-operative defiance under the pretense of conformity. It is not the cold that are most nauseating to the Lord, but the lukewarm. These are the sinners who try to avoid the consequences of their defiance without ceasing to be defiant. Theirs is a pseudo-submission to God's Spirit, as they continue undercover to hold back. Behind their apparent devotion they are seeking the greatest personal advantage, without burning any of their bridges. They are interested in "losing their life" only because they hope thereby to "find it." Luther sees this pseudo-piety as again the sin against the First Commandment, "because they do not seek the things of God, but their own, even in God Himself and His saints, and they are their own ultimate end and idol of this work of theirs, using God, enjoying themselves."[8]

We have a crude example of this camouflaged defiance in Ibsen's character of Peer Gynt. Peer Gynt could never move himself to sin courageously because he feared the consequences. He made his money sending shiploads of idols each spring to China and soothed his conscience by sending missionaries to China each autumn. At the close of his life he compared himself to an onion he was peeling. As layer after layer peeled off he searched for the kernel but there was none. He was all layers and no core. He had no soul. Although he did many things in many places, each was a series in a cycle going nowhere, and his life ended in the despair of one lost in the woods who discovers with horror that he is back where he started. He ended up with the Button Moulder. Because he was neither an ardent sinner nor a serious believer, his soul was fitted for nothing so decisive as hell, or heaven, but only for the casting ladle for buttons.

**VI.
Distorted
in the
Highest**

The interpretation of sin as defiance—and worse, defiance trying to appear as something other—cuts across any so-called division between a higher and lower nature of man. The idea that we sin with our lower nature while our higher nature strives after virtue is an importation of Greek thought into Christian circles. From a Christian point of view man is a whole, and as a whole is either under God's wrath or under God's grace. In the words of Luther, "He whom God receives, he completely re-

ceives, and he whom he favors he completely favors. On
the other hand, he is angry at the whole of him with
whom he is angry."[9] Since the individual person is a unity,
his position of defiance exists in his higher and lower
natures. In his highest capacities as a human being he
remains distorted, because as an egotist he is curved in
upon himself—*incurvatus in se.* Being distorted as a person he distorts what he could learn about religion and
morality from nature. Who could surpass the Greeks for
wisdom so far as man is concerned? Yet so far as Aristotle
could perceive, virtue was enlightened self-interest. And
so far as Socrates could discern, sin was ignorance. But
one who saw more clearly said, "Whoever knows what
is right to do and fails to do it, for him it is sin" (James
4:17). Here again we confront the paradoxical nature of
original sin. As natural creatures we are predestined to
distort because our vision is distorted from within. We
need revelation even to know how distorted we are. It
takes a Kierkegaard to surpass his hero Socrates on this
point.

> The natural man, the pagan, thinks thus: "O well, I
> admit that I have not understood everything in heaven
> and earth; if there is to be a revelation, let it inform
> us about the heavenly; but that there should be a reve-
> lation to explain what sin is, that is the most preposter-
> ous thing of all. I don't pretend to be a perfect man,
> far from it, but I know and I am willing to concede how
> far I am from perfection—ought I not then to know
> what sin is?" But Christianity makes answer, "No, that
> is what you know least about, how far you are from
> perfection, and what sin is." Behold, in this sense, in a
> Christian sense, sin doubtless is ignorance, it is igno-
> rance of what sin is.[10]

In our distortion we are concerned about the wrong sins,
afraid of the wrong things, and worried about the wrong

people. We see the outside world distortedly because we see ourselves distortedly. If we could see ourselves as we really are, it would seem as strange as is the sound of our own voice when we first hear it on tape. The reaction to one's personality profile from a test such as the Minnesota Multiphasic Personality Inventory is often one of disbelief. However, after a twenty-minute discussion with the interpretor, the skeptic usually begins to acknowledge the validity of the test. Is the initial rejection due primarily to defenses we erect to protect distortions in our own self-image or to a genuine ignorance of who we are? This distortion is the greatest hindrance to our sanctification, since our very nature is in active (though subconscious) resistance to the truth.

VII. Distortion of Guilt   The distorting influence extends also to the sense of guilt. When our guilt is distorted by egotism we are concerned primarily about the mental image of us that others have—especially the Very Important People in our lives, including God. This concern prods us to seek first the improvement of this mental image of ourselves in others, rather than the kingdom of God and his righteousness. So we miss the whole idea of *sola gratia*—that we are received by God as an unmerited blessing—primarily because this good news of *sola gratia* is the *skandalon,* the offense, to human pride. Since the Christian also has the flesh that "lusteth" against the Spirit, the good news is an offense also to him. His guilt then is a matter of hurt pride or discouragement that he has not achieved this idealized image of himself so that he could "think more highly of himself." His idealized image is actually an idolized image.

In reality this is guilt before the superego into which the conscience has become distorted. In Freud's interpretation of the superego, the mores of the group are internalized to become a part of the self. Pressure then comes from the superego to follow these mores to gain acceptance and avoid rejection. This superego distortion of the conscience is a hindrance to a relationship with God because it is based upon the need to assure ourselves of status in the eyes of others—a need that is more compulsive and self-defensive than religious.

Are we then concerned with a purely psychological phenomenon in superego guilt? To divide the human being into a psychological level and a spiritual level is to return to the age-old Greek tendency to divide us into parts—a tendency that does violence to the view that man is a totality—that his "parts" are submerged in his wholeness. Since the divine-human encounter is relevant to all human disturbances, psychological problems have a religious dimension. The tendency to divide spiritual (religious) activities from psychological (secular) activities leads to a superficial view of sin. The distinction between religious and secular activities removes much of our common life from its religious significance. So also the separation of psychological from spiritual removes much of our common life from its sinful significance. It tends to focus on sin in its observable manifestations rather than on the thoughts and intents of the heart. It leads to distinctions such as mortal and venial, which, though having some justification, tend to return to a rule book type of morality which fails to recognize sin as ever-present defiance. Actually sin is not in opposition to morality but to faith. "Whatever does not proceed from faith is sin" (Rom. 14:23).

The events of the secular day which have little ecclesiastical meaning may still have meaning for the development of the self. For this reason religion cannot be simply one activity among others in a person's life. Whatever affects the development of the self is of religious concern. Take the matter of disposition for example. Shall a burst of anger in a daily irritation be viewed as inconsequential religiously or shall it be subjected to a religious evaluation? When *religion* is separated from the *secular,* one might shrug off anger as merely "blowing one's top." When religion is taken into all of life, this same anger may be viewed as a presumptuous act in which one individual arrogantly takes it upon himself to abuse another. Whatever sentiment of respect for the personality of others that might have been present within him is overcome by his anger. The conduct that results is precisely the kind that Paul says is not *agape,* love. "Agape is not irritable or resentful; . . . it is not arrogant or rude"—it is not disrespectful of personality.

However, the person involved may be one who normally holds things inside of himself, and "blowing his top" may be a step in the direction of his personal growth. The expression of his anger, then, would be the lesser of two evils. The fact that it is necessary for his self-development does not remove this moral judgment. In our complex existence the choice is often between a greater and a lesser evil rather than between evil and good. In spite of this fact, it is essential for sanctification that not only the lesser evil be chosen but that all behavior be morally identified.

We come now to the problem of whether the distorted guilt of the superego is simply a primitive form of guilt or whether it is on a tangent from genuine guilt. The scrupulous, tyrannized superego of the perfectionist is certainly not unrelated to guilt before God. It is an expression of the tension between the way we are and the way we should be, and this tension is at the heart of the religious quest. On the other hand, the very nature of the perfectionist superego is an obstacle to God. It is one thing to aim for perfection, but it is another to abuse ourselves for our failure to achieve it. Because his conscience demands that he fulfill an idealized image of himself, the perfectionist can never accept himself as he is. By this token he disrespects himself. Because he is under the law rather than under grace, he bypasses forgiveness in favor of self-punishment. Although his goal of perfection is unrealizable, it remains the only basis upon which he can accept himself. For one who is accepted upon the basis of God's grace, the goal of perfection is a challenge growing out of his acceptance. The agony of the perfectionist is not the creative agony of sanctification. Rather it is the agony of one who needs this agony to tolerate his own existence. As a distortion, the conscience of the superego is off on a tangent, and yet when it is exposed to the "baptism of the Holy Spirit," its sensitivity to moral values is an asset in the development of genuine guilt. Only now this sensitivity becomes the basis for a love-dominated rather than a fear-dominated conscientiousness.

Hatred of sin is necessary for the determination to overcome it. It is essential that all of life be accountable to God—that the whole self stand guilty before God. The overcoming of sin is God's work. For that matter, so is the hating which is the first step in overcoming. But God works through human activity. Psychological and sociological interpretations of the *how* and *why* of sin should be a help in overcoming sin because they enlist the faculties of our intelligence. Certainly an understanding of our emotional predispositions and our environmental exasperations is a *must* in any intelligent confrontation of our deficiencies. How else can we penetrate beyond the rationalizations and repressions by which we try to hide our defiance and into the environmental circumstances and human relationships which clarify our behavior?

Yet it is precisely because of this explanatory feature

VIII. Hatred and Conquest

that these sciences of human behavior may be more of a hindrance than a help. The gravity of sin is obviously minimized when it is explained by factors other than our own responsibility. The implication of the explanations is that basically each of us is good—that we mean well—but there are extenuating circumstances. So we are back to flesh as weakness to the exclusion of flesh as defiance. The more such understanding helps one to see himself as a victim of circumstances, the more it helps to reduce his hatred of his sinfulness. The result is that this wisdom from the sciences which could be the greatest of modern assets to the overcoming of sin may instead be the most formidable of modern obstructions.

The counselee who has "read up" in psychology often proves to be a most difficult counselee. He may already have arrived at some psychological interpretation of his problem, and even be quite accurate in his diagnosis. In reality, however, he is more interested in diagnosing his problem than in solving it. If he can give it a name, it reduces the mystery and hence the fear. This bypass into the realm of intellectual comprehension is for him the escape route from the pain of catharsis. Instead of using his intellect to confront his total person, he has used it to avoid this confrontation. By using his psychological knowledge to "intellectualize" his problem, he illustrates how easily this knowledge of the sciences can become a way of escape from the pain of judgment and the responsibility for effort. Understanding in itself is not the equivalent of healing. Only as it leads to courageous effort does understanding fulfill its therapeutic role. By itself it is simply the current fad of the dilettante, an obstruction rather than a means for healing.

Only as this understanding from the sciences is interpreted in terms of our own inexcusable and defiant ego-

tism can it be the "handmaid of the Lord"—that is, only
as it is integrated into a realistic understanding of sin. For
overcoming sin means overcoming this defiant egotism.
This occurs when the self is committed beyond itself to
God. From the philosopher Santayana's point of view this
would be genuine piety. Says Santayana, "Piety is man's
reverent attachment to the sources of his being and the
steadying of his life by that attachment."[11] This piety is
expressed in the desire to bless God rather than the desire
that God bless us. It moves us to direct our lives to his
glory. We use such language so glibly in our churches
that we become dulled to the fact that blessing God is the
most impossible of activities for human nature. The fact
that we can say it so easily indicates how much our piety
amounts to mere verbalization. While we desire God's
kingdom to come, we desire that it come through us, and
our interest is in proportion to our role. While we insist
we do not want credit, we show by our critical attitude
toward those who are receiving the credit how much our
attitude belies our words.

John the Baptist did not escape the common conflict
between the flesh and the Spirit. Therefore we have some
appreciation of the struggle behind the statement attributed to him—"He must increase, but I must decrease"
(John 3:30). Yet his victory was not assured when he
said it—he also had to live it. Paul too was bedeviled by
egotism. Therefore we can put ourselves into his place as
he was confronted by fellow pastors who were saying
disparaging things about him. But his solution to the
matter shows his awareness of a higher devotion.

> Some indeed preach Christ from envy and rivalry,
> but others from good will. The latter do it out of love,
> knowing that I am put here for the defense of the
> gospel; the former proclaim Christ out of partisan-

ship, not sincerely but thinking to afflict me in my im-
prisonment. What then? Only that in every way,
whether in pretense or in truth, Christ is proclaimed;
and in that I rejoice (Phil. 1:15-18).

Desiring God's glory comes close to what Jesus described
as desiring the Holy Spirit. "If you then, who are evil,
know how to give good gifts to your children, how much
more will the heavenly Father give the Holy Spirit to those
who ask him?" (Luke 11:13). But the point is, who is
asking for the Holy Spirit? Yet Jesus speaks as though he
could assume this to be the top priority in our requests.

The Holy Spirit is the person of the Trinity whom
Christian theology associates with sanctification. The fact
that sanctification is looked upon as the work of the Holy
Spirit helps us to acknowledge a disturbing problem. How
can the self be committed beyond itself to God when it
is a self-centered self? How can the proud will overcome
pride? We are face to face with the finite side of our freedom—the helpless side of our responsibility—the frustra-
ting agony of our guilt. We are confronted full force in
this existential dilemma by the paradox of original sin.
I am responsible, and yet I am helpless. I am obligated to
God, and yet I am enslaved to my own self-deification. I
am called of God and predestined to defiance. I am guilty
—but hopelessly guilty. To desire the Holy Spirit is to
desire—to long for—the grace of God to overcome this
deadlocked ambivalence in my soul. What we are able
to do shall have to be done for us, and what is done for
us is what we shall be able to do. For to desire the Holy
Spirit is to desire God for God's own sake—to seek his
glory. Such sanctification does not come about lightly—
if it comes at all. In fact, it comes through the process
of dying.

Footnotes

1. *The Confessions of St. Augustine* (London: Fontana Books, 1959), p. 210.
2. *Ibid.*, p. 210-211.
3. Søren Kierkegaard, *The Sickness unto Death*. Trans. by Walter Lowrie (New York: Doubleday and Co., 1954), p. 228.
4. Martin Luther, "Against Latomus," *Luther's Works* (Philadelphia: Muhlenberg Press, 1958), Vol. 32, p. 183.
5. Reinhold Niebuhr, *The Nature and Destiny of Man* (New York: Scribners, 1953), Vol. II, p. 43.
6. Gordon Rupp, *The Righteousness of God* (New York: Philosophical Library, 1953), p. 167.
7. Cf. Philip Watson, *Let God Be God* (London: Epworth Press, 1947), p. 16.
8. *Ibid.*, p. 89.
9. Luther, "Against Latomus," *op. cit.*, p. 228.
10. Kierkegaard, *op. cit.*, p. 226.
11. George Santayana, *Reason in Religion* (London: Constable & Co., 1905), p. 179.

CHAPTER THREE

His Righteousness or Ours

If spiritual growth means growing away from something, namely sin, it also means growing toward something, namely righteousness. As Christendom has not always been of one mind regarding an understanding of sin, so we find a similar divergence of interpretation regarding righteousness. There is general agreement that sin is overcome through the Gospel of Christ, but how the Gospel accomplishes this is another matter. Some would say that overcoming is the natural follow-up to forgiveness, as the believer responds in gratitude to the warmth of divine love. Others would see it as a matter of trying and striving to do better through whatever resources the Gospel makes available. Still others consider the development of our own righteousness as essential for our salvation.

Even if we could obtain agreement through a few carefully worded propositions, the difference in emphasis would remain, and it is this difference, rather than carefully worded agreements, that reflects the distinctive characteristics of church bodies. Because of the elusive nature of sanctification it is doubtful whether any one group has the correct formula for the overcoming of sin. In fact, it is doubtful whether there is any such formula.

There is a biblical description of how sin is overcome in Paul's Letter to the Romans. In the first eight chapters the Apostle describes how the Gospel of Christ changes human nature. In the first two chapters he makes much of the fact that God has revealed himself to man from the beginning through his creation. Therefore, Gentiles as well as Jews have no defense for their conduct, for they are aware of the judgment that accompanies their actions. Although the Gentiles do not have the written code as do the Jews, the Apostle maintains that they show by their awareness of right and wrong that they have the law inscribed on their hearts. In fact, the true Jew is not known by any outward accouterments but by the inner workings of God's Spirit upon the heart. Those who follow the inner directives of this "circumcision of the heart" by persistence in welldoing shall receive eternal life, but those who refuse obedience to God's law shall receive their just retribution. In either instance the consequence is to the Jew first but also to the Gentile. In fact, the Jew should beware lest his religious advantage cause him to criticize the conduct of Gentiles, for those who sit in judgment condemn also themselves, for the judge is guilty of doing the very things for which he criticizes others.

In spite of what appears to be an obvious opportunity for all to obey the law of God, Paul insists that judgment has passed on all, for all have broken this law. Rather than bringing justification in the sight of God the law brings only the consciousness of sin. What then? Here is where Paul brings in the Gospel. There is another way of justification—witnessed by both Moses and the prophets—effective through Christ for all who believe. This is the good

I.
The
Gospel
in
Romans

news—that we can be justified by faith apart from what we have been able or unable to do in keeping the law.

Is then faith used to undermine obedience to the law? Certainly not! Rather, through faith we are really making the law more secure. Because of our carnality, the law which is spiritual is impotent to accomplish its purpose. Nor does Paul think there is anything revolutionary about this justification by faith. Abraham, the father of the old covenant, was himself justified by faith. When all seemed hopeless so far as the natural processes for reproduction were concerned, Abraham continued to believe that God would fulfill his promise to raise up a posterity out of his marriage, through which all the nations of the earth would be blessed. And it was this faith—this leap in faith —that was reckoned to him as righteousness.

This posterity which God raised up from Abraham and Sarah climaxed its blessing to the nations in the coming of the Christ, who "was delivered to death for our misdeeds and raised to life to justify us" (Rom. 4:25 NEB). He came to rectify the harm caused by the universal disobedience of the ages. In fact, Paul sees him as the new Adam whose obedience more than compensates for the disobedience of the first Adam. For if the wrongdoing of the first Adam brought death in its wake, he asks, how much more shall the righteousness of the new Adam bring life through grace! For it was while we were still set in opposition to God that Christ entered into death for us. Here, then, is the ultimate overture of love. If the death of Christ is the act of love that reconciles us to God, it is the life of Christ—his risen presence—that sanctifies us. For if the disobedience of the first Adam made many to be sinners, so the obedience of the new Adam will make many to be righteous.

Descriptions—even descriptions of God's redemptive activity—can remain abstractions. But for Paul justifica-

tion by faith *involves* us. Not only did Christ die for us
—we also die! The man we once were is crucified *with*
Christ. Therefore the sinful self is dead—even buried as
Baptism indicates, so that the new self can come to life—
resurrected with Christ. In all of this the Apostle draws
no difference between the forgiveness of sin and the overcoming of sin, for in becoming reconciled to God we have
died to sin. Since we are no longer under the law but
under grace, we are free to serve God in the new self
according to the inner Spirit rather than the outer code.

So, then, in Paul's judgment the law which was supposed to lead to life actually leads to death because our
sinful self finds in the judgment of the law an opportunity
to enslave us to sin. The fact that we are slaves is shown
in our unwillingness even to acknowledge our sinful self
as belonging to us. We find ourselves in the predicament
of doing what we detest. This brings us to the ultimate
of frustration that leads to the bottom of despair. "The
good that I would, I do not, and the evil which I would
not, that I do. Miserable creature that I am, who shall
deliver me from this wretched state of existence!" It is at
this existential moment of total defeat that the Gospel is
really the good news. "I thank God! Deliverance is through
Christ our Lord!"

The conflict can be summed up by saying that the self-
that-I-identify-with is subject to God's law, but the self-
I-disown continues to serve sin. But for the Apostle the
decisive issue is settled—there is no condemnation under
the law for those who are justified by faith in Christ. For
Christ took upon himself our own nature and suffered
this human conflict to the bitter end, and in his triumph
over sin he has broken the hold of sin over all those who
look to him for their redemption. Again this is no abstract
arrangement, for those who by faith are justified receive
God's own Spirit. It is this presence of the Spirit within

us that assures us of victory, for it is by the Spirit that we put to death the self that is opposed to God.

But for Paul the Spirit is not simply power—he is also love and affection. It is he who draws us to God as a child is drawn to his parents, moving us with warmth of feeling to say, Father! Because of the security in such a relationship we have the assurance that regardless of the sufferings we endure in bearing with evil internally and externally, the final outcome will be beatitude beyond description. The victory we have now by faith makes us all the more anxious for the fulfillment of this faith in the coming climax of redemption. For the Apostle, faith and hope go together, not faith and sight.

But this faith is not only for the future. Even now Paul believes that the Spirit functions for us in the midst of our weakness. When we seem unable even to pray, connections are not broken, for the Spirit prays for us and because of this continuous tie of intercession we know that all things—even our weaknesses—shall work together for the ultimate good. For God has determined from all eternity that we should be conformed to the image of his Son. It is out of this foreordination that we have been called, and having been called, have been justified, and having been justified, shall also be sanctified. For it is the believer's conviction, his faith, that nothing—nothing in all creation—can sever the relationship of love established with God for us through the redemptive work of Christ. Thus the Apostle brings to a triumphant climax his treatise on the victory over sin.

II. Sanctification by Crucifixion and Resurrection

According to Romans, redemption comes out of conflict. In fact, if there were no conflict, it is doubtful if there could be any redemption. Although this conflict is developed in Romans in terms of the Christian experience, it is a conflict that is not confined to this experience.

Judging by his description of man's natural state, Paul considered this conflict as universal. However, in man's natural state the conflict is distorted. Man lacks the hope that would encourage him to penetrate to the depths of his conflict. In his own defense he considers it a conflict between his higher and his lower natures. Though the conflict is distorted it creates the dissatisfaction and discomfort necessary to open him to receive help.

But it is only in the milieu of the religious experience that the conflict can reach the proportions of reality. We need the assurance of hope before we can muster the courage to face the conflict in its deeper dimensions. In this perspective we see the conflict as not only between a higher and a lower nature, but as the conflict between our total self and the righteousness of God. Without faith this glimpse into the depths would plunge us into a despair which we could neither endure nor cease to endure. But with faith there is also hope that converts this despair into repentance. It is this hope that makes possible the awareness of sin. Without it we could go little farther than Socrates—that sin is ignorance; with it we can go on with the New Testament to the realization that sin is defiance. For Christ has taken the common conflict of humanity and endured it in its full and undistorted anguish so that humanity in facing the conflict might lay hold on redemption. Because we are protected by the Gospel, we can enter into the depths of the conflict, and through the leap of faith experience healing not only on the surface but also from within.

In penetrating to the bottom of the conflict we experience the collapse of everything but this hope of the Gospel. All formulas for control and all defenses for concealment are defunct. Nor is there any hidden reserve that may avail for such emergencies. Rather, we are purged of all props, supports, reserves, and even all illusions, for these belong to the realm of sight. As such they are sub-stitutes for faith, and in their collapse only the leap in faith remains. Through this experience all that belongs to the old man in his higher and lower natures is crucified.

In the practice of pastoral care our resistance to such crucifixion often comes to light. We are loath to call upon our last resource for fear that it may not be sufficient. Then what? The very despair created by this question is enough to make us content with our illusions and deter-mined to hold to them. To perpetuate the illusion that he could make good grades if he really tried, a student may consistently resist doing his best in order to have an excuse for failure that does not reflect on his basic ability. If he can excuse himself by saying that he did not study for the test or that he really is not interested in the course, he is accounting for his failures in a way that does not reflect upon his native ability. By saving face he hopes to preserve his essential worth. To really study for a test, to admit that he desires to do well, and then to fail—this is the most humiliating experience of all. What now can he say except that he evidently does not have what it takes. Actually this fear of inadequacy was lurking in the shadows of his mind all along.

The same thing may occur in the realm of personality. A person may hold himself back from relating to others. He may even withdraw when overtures of friendship are made to him. He rationalizes by saying that he is not in-terested or that these people bore him or irritate him. What he really fears is to expose himself to a close rela-tionship and be hurt. Obviously it has already happened in his life, and the spurn that he received has been so humiliating to his self-respect that the only defense is never to expose himself again. His basic fear is that if people learn to know him as he really is, they will finally tire of him and reject him. In preference to this the illusion of not caring is more attractive.

The experience of crucifixion is never pleasant, nor is it sought. It is the death of our acceptable self, our righteous self, the self of which we are proud. This leaves us in despair, for we know no other resource. Our best has been tried and found wanting. This throws us afresh on the grace of God alone. The Spirit whom we receive enables us to believe in God's victory in the face of our own defeats. What results is an acceptance of ourselves without props. This is unconditional acceptance, and unconditional acceptance is genuine acceptance. Because this acceptance is extended to the total self, healing can take place from within. The crucifixion of the old man forces us to relinquish the supports of sight so that faith can emerge. This faith belongs to the new man who is sustained by hope—hope made possible by the resurrection of Christ.

The acceptance that we experience in the resurrection of hope is deeply personal. Because the love of God is characterized by tenderness as well as by sacrifice, the parental nature of his acceptance is as warm as it is total. The hope that converts despair into repentance is inseparable from the relationship that is created through acceptance. The security that is ours through this relationship is sustained not only by acceptance but by affection. In our day of existentialism this factor is often overlooked. The important role played by the Sacraments in the reception of God's acceptance emphasizes the tangible nature of his love. It is given by touch as well as by word. Consequently, our response is not only commitment but gratitude. There is warmth as well as awe in the divine-human encounter. God is not only obeyed—he is loved.

When the threats have been reduced we can see things more clearly. Even the value of the crucifixion experience is perceived. The conviction grows that all things work together for the ultimate good. Although a "grievous" experience, the crucifixion of the old man offers a wealth of insight to the new man. We have been humbled rather than humiliated. Insight comes from that which is humbling, and is blocked by that which is humiliating. The difference between the two is hope. Hope makes the difference between a wounded and a crucified pride. A wounded pride, like a wounded animal, is dangerous. It takes the Gospel to make the Law effective. Thus wisdom becomes the possession of the humble and folly of the proud.

These negative experiences may not always be resolved. Instead of becoming aware of their meaningfulness, one may continue to see only their meaninglessness. As a result, they become infected with despair and may be too painful even to think about. Rather than being preludes to growth, they become detours or even barricades to growth. Pastoral counseling is the ministry that is designed to help remove these barricades. The purpose of pastoral counseling is not simply to assist the person to talk about the negative experience, but rather to relive it. This means that he relates the experience through reenactment even to the original emotions. Like the testimony of the anonymous alcoholic at his weekly meeting, this reliving may need to be done more than once when the recollection is very painful. Each time he relives it, however, he dies a little more to the fear and to the hurt and to the humiliation. Gradually he begins to detect a glimmer of meaning or purpose—actually providence—in the pain of the past. God becomes larger as the threat becomes smaller. In being able to accept the experience, he is resurrected from its death. The way has been opened for new growth.

From our secure position in the resurrection we can reflect upon the significance of our crucifixion. As the immediacy of the pain subsides, the factors involved in producing the pain come to light. We begin to realize what led to the fall, and why the fall was distasteful. The result is a growing awareness of its salutary effect. We needed this insight into ourselves in order to grow. Our fall was inevitable, even as it was necessary. God has succeeded in getting through to us, and we are better prepared for the future.

Again the dialogue of pastoral counseling provides insight into this experience. A highly successful man had experienced a loss in self-confidence to the extent that he could no longer stand up to criticism. His faith had always meant a great deal to him, but this too had deteriorated. The only clue to his problem was that he had been taken suddenly ill several months previously and had become ineligible for a promotion for which he had hoped. We break into his observations at this point.

Man: My faith has always meant much to me—perhaps because my home life was so poor. I set my goal—worked hard for it—and would make it. This has happened over and over again.

Pastor: But it didn't happen this last time.

Man: No—I got sick—and was disqualified. I guess I wasn't up to the disappointment.

Pastor: Seemed as if God had let you down that time.

Man: Yeah—couldn't see much future after that.

Pastor: This was a new experience for your faith.

Man: It collapsed it. (pause) I suppose it was inevitable. Sooner or later it had to happen.

Pastor: But when it happened you would be in for trouble.

Man: For a while I thought my whole world had ended. But I'm beginning to see that it really hasn't. I'll have to admit there is plenty of challenge in my present job if I could accept it. Who knows—maybe God knew what he was doing.

But the security of the resurrection is a security by faith. There is no assurance of any gradual and steady ascent. The next step forward may be down—down to a fresh revelation of what sin is—down to a new defeat for our pride—down to another crucifixion of our flesh. This is not the way we would like it. Yet it is the way by which the Spirit of God conforms us to the image of the crucified and risen Christ. To this we are destined—foreordained. The fact remains, however, that the thought of these successive sufferings of soul in our lives can be too much for us. Surely there is some easier may. Would we not receive enough wisdom through a few of these dying experiences, enough holiness, so that the cycle could cease? So long as we are "in the flesh" the crucifixion experience is the only way of defeating the old Adam. The conflict between a higher and a lower nature in man is now seen as a conflict between an old and a new man, a conflict between the flesh and the Spirit, for the new man lives in rapport with the Spirit.

As seen by Paul, Baptism is the sacramental expression of this conformity to Christ. "Do you not know that all of us who have been baptized into Christ Jesus were baptized into his death? We were buried therefore with him by baptism into death, so that as Christ was raised from the dead by the glory of the Father, we too might walk in newness of life" (Rom. 6:3, 4). In Baptism we are crucified with Christ and with him risen from the dead. Though performed but once, Baptism is existential in its application. As a mediator of the covenant of grace, it is the anchor of our hope. Luther's answer to the catechetical question, "What does Baptism mean for daily living?" shows his appreciation of its dynamic nature. "It means that our sinful self, with all its evil deeds and desires, should be drowned through daily repentance; and that day after day a new self should arise to live with God in

righteousness and purity forever." Emphasis is on the
idea that this occurs *daily*. The baptismal covenant is not
only remembered, it is relived as we repent in the present
and begin anew the risen life.

Differentiating between justification and sanctification
has been a source of tension throughout the history of the
church. Are justification and sanctification two separate
and distinctive functions of God's Spirit? Or are they
better understood when they are viewed as different dimensions of a single process? Is the human will involved
more in sanctification than in justification? Or are both
solely the work of grace? Is it possible to separate them
too much? Or is the danger in combining them?

*III.
Sanctification
Through
Justification*

Actually it is as artificial to separate justification and
sanctification as it is hazardous to confuse them. From the
perspective of pastoral theology it is obvious that the same
experience that justifies also sanctifies. Even as there can
be no sanctification until there has been justification, so
the very occurrence of justification is a sanctifying influence. The forgivenss of sin is not the prerequisite for
the overcoming of sin; it *is* the overcoming of sin—and
justification is effected through forgiveness. The justification experience sanctifies. As forgiveness is bestowed in
the baptismal covenant and renewed at each expression
of repentance, so justification occurs in the baptismal covenant and is renewed at each reassurance of forgiveness.
Baptism, then, is relived repeatedly. Existentially we are
redeemed by being put to death with Christ to the old
and being resurrected with Christ to the new, and our
growth in this redemption is by this same process. The
law breaks down the old man so that the Gospel can build
up the new man. The means by which the Christian life
comes into being is also the means by which it develops.

Since the justifying experience is also the sanctifying

experience, the pastoral approach to the redeemed and to the unredeemed is essentially the same. Any approach that opens a person to the Holy Spirit's justification would also open him to the Spirit's sanctification. A pastoral care which differentiates the redeemed from the unredeemed in its approach commits the theological error that spiritual growth occurs after forgiveness rather than through it. Though there is obviously a difference between the redeemed and the unredeemed—even an ultimate difference —it is not our differentiation to make. Nor is it a differentiation that removes the redeemed from the common human lot. While the redeemed have the Spirit, they also have the flesh. Though the internal conflict is distorted in the unredeemed, it is still related to the conflict in the redeemed—and the remedy for this conflict is the same for both. The redeemed need forgiveness as do the unredeemed. They also are offended by the Gospel. This Gospel that converts the unredeemed continues to convert the redeemed—just as the law that condemns the flesh in the unredeemed condemns it also in the redeemed. The same forgiveness that reconciles the unredeemed to God renews this reconciliation in the redeemed. As much as it may offend our need to see progress, the fact remains that the way of growth is by crucifixion and resurrection —by repentance and forgiveness.

If we attempt to differentiate the redeemed by the way they talk or by the way they act, we perpetuate the cleavage between the Pharisee and the publican. Those classified as the redeemed may even acknowledge that they need forgiveness, but surely less of it than the publicans. Yet it was the publican who Jesus said went down to his house justified. Those who are redeemed therefore never graduate from the experience of the publican. Otherwise they would become as unredeemed as the Pharisee. The publican's smiting of his breast and his cry,

"God be merciful to me, a sinner," are indications of his crucifixion. His going to his house justified is an expression of his resurrection. The way of the publican is the way of entering and the way of continuing in God's kingdom— the way of justification for the sinner and the way of sanctification for the saint.

The reconciliation effected by each occurrence of repentance is a reconciliation within an already existing union. The way of growth is within the dynamic of relationship. For this reason the divine-human relationship has its closest analogy in the most intimate of human relationships. In the Old and the New Testaments the relationship between God and Israel and between Christ and his church is compared to the relationship between husband and wife. This analogy affords us an insight into what our relationship with God is like because of our familiarity with the marriage relationship. The relationship between Christ and his church also provides us a picture of what marriage can potentially become.

In both marriage and religion there is always the danger of idealism. Because of our romantic notions about marriage and about religion we may be unable to integrate the inevitable tensions in either of these areas into our idealism. Either we end up in despair or we repress the tension. Because it constitutes too great a threat to our idealistic image of married life and of the religious life, what could be the potential for a more significant relationship in either becomes the means only for weakening the relationship. The ups and downs in married life need not be simply cycles of meaningless repetition any more than the ups and down in our relationship to God. Nor need the tensions they produce rupture the union. Rather they may lead to reconciliations which result in a deeper and more meaningful relationship.

The need to see meaning in the events of life is fundamental to Logotherapy as set forth by Viktor Frankl. According to this school of psychotherapy, man does not invent his own meaning but rather he detects it. Therefore he does not fulfill himself when he discovers this meaning, but rather he transcends himself. The problem today is that man sees no such meaning in his life, but rather sees only disappointment, disillusion, suffering without purpose, a cycle of futility. His is an existential vacuum brought on by the anxiety of meaninglessness which the present-day theologian sees as the contemporary expression of the accusing work of the law. The vacuum is the judgment upon our broken relationships—our broken covenants. Meaning is restored when relationships are restored. "The salvation of man," says Frankl, "is through love and in love."[1]

Frankl's contribution to psychotherapy is comparable to Luther's contribution to theology in that the insights of both came to them through suffering. Luther's inner agony over his salvation has its counterpart in Frankl's agony for survival in the Nazi concentration camps. The words that became existential for Frankl through this terrifying experience were those of Nietzsche: "He who has a *why* to live for can bear with almost any *how*." For Luther it was the word of Paul, "The just shall live by faith."

Though stripped of everything except his "naked existence," Frankl realized that his captors could not take away the last of the freedoms—the freedom to choose his own attitude toward his sufferings. This was not only his privilege, it was his responsibility. "The way in which a man takes up his cross gives him ample opportunity—even under the most difficult circumstances—to add a deeper meaning to his life."[2]

Was Frankl's realization of his naked existence, the collapse of all previous supports and defenses, a "hitting bottom" where one either discovers the "hidden God" or bogs down in anguish of despair? Frankl describes his discovery in religious terms. "I went down on my knees. At that moment there was very little I knew of myself or of the world—I had but one sentence in mind—always the same: 'I called to the Lord from my narrow prison and He answered me in the freedom of space.' How long I knelt there and repeated this sentence memory can no longer recall. But I know that on that day, in that hour, my new life started."[3]

God's acceptance is redemptive because he takes the unacceptable seriously. He cares. His grace is not a cheapened grace which lightly dismisses sin. Such forgiveness would be of little moment. A covenant based upon it would be more a transaction of ideas than a relationship of persons. It would not involve us enough to elicit a response. Unfortunately our eagerness to proclaim the Gospel often causes us to proclaim it in such an indulgent manner that the hearer could well reason, "Shall we continue in sin that grace may abound?" This is always the reaction when grace is cheapened through indulgence.

God does more than bestow a favor in granting forgiveness. Because of the gravity of the human predicament he had to identify himself with this predicament. He shares our lot in becoming the sacrifice for sin. In taking upon himself our sin, he made it possible for us to take upon ourselves his righteousness. By his incarnation he humbled himself to come in the likeness of men. For our sakes he became not only a man but a servant of men. He who had no sin of his own was made to be sin for us that we might in turn receive from him the righteousness of his sacrifice. His righteousness extended to the suffering of the cross, where his cry, "My God, my God why hast thou forsaken me?" climaxed an obedience that had tasted death—spiritual death—for every man.

Here was the atonement. The Son of Man identified himself with the existential agony of abandonment. Jesus *felt* it—forsaken by God and rejected by man—in the torment of pain.

Confronted by such a demonstration of divine concern, we can scarcely be unmoved. Love that is exhibited in sacrifice and suffering elicits a response—if not gratitude, at least guilt. But the response that is evoked is not a substitute for Christ's righteousness but rather a result of it. Redemption is more than the bestowal of forgiveness —it is the bestowal of righteousness. Forgiveness removes the barrier of evil. But more is needed than the removal of evil. Even as the Son of Man became sin for us, so also he became our righteousness. Where the first Adam succumbed to the tempter, the new Adam triumphed, and by his triumph he established for humanity a new righteousness. Although tempted in all points as we are, he emerged the victor—though by the anguish of bloody sweat.

The doctrine of Christ's righteousness is highly relevant to the struggles we encounter in life. If there is anything we need in these struggles, it is the assurance that we are loved unconditionally—that this love does not depend upon the outcome of the struggle. The bestowal of Christ's righteousness is the evidence, not only that God takes sin seriously, but that he loves us unconditionally. The conditions had to be reckoned with. The law had to be fulfilled. Otherwise life could not be taken seriously— it could have no real meaning. Obedience is not only recommended, it is demanded. Forgiveness is one thing; fulfillment is another. If we dismiss the law, we dismiss also any meaning in life. By fulfilling the law, Christ preserved the seriousness of forgiveness. God's love is unconditional, not because he dismisses the conditions but because he fulfills them. Here is a justification that transcends not only our own evil but also our own good.

Throughout the history of the church there have been many who have objected to this doctrine of the imputation of righteousness. Their chief objection is that imputing Christ's righteousness to the believer discourages him from developing his own righteousness. Those of Catholic persuasion are disturbed by any doctrine that seems to impute but not to regenerate. The same is true of evangelicals who lay heavy emphasis upon sanctification. John Wesley, for example, viewed this doctrine as a threat to his own emphasis on sanctification. Actually the imputation of righteousness stimulates rather than hinders sanctification. It provides us with the security that we need before we can seek anything for other than egocentric reasons. Righteousness begins with the motive. As important as our actions are, they can stem from varying motivations. Yet only the motivation of love makes an action righteous in the eyes of God.

Before we can love another we must be released from anxiety over ourselves. It is this that the imputation of Christ's righteousness accomplishes. It frees us from anxiety over our own salvation so that we can devote our energies to the salvation of others. Since we are justified in God's sight on the basis of Christ's righteousness, we are released from the obligation to qualify in his sight by our own righteousness. The moment we use our own righteousness to obtain God's favor, it ceases to be righteousness. It is corrupted at its source by egocentricity. In contrast to the centripetal motion of egocentric activity, the motion of love is centrifugal. The doctrine of imputation allows our relationship with Christ to depend upon his stable righteousness rather than our unstable righteousness. Here is the basis for the security that makes it possible to love. It releases us from the defensive need to turn into ourselves, so that we can turn outward to our neighbor.

The righteousness of Christ, therefore, is necessary for the genuineness of our own righteousness. When our tie with God is threatened by our ever-present conflict between the flesh and the Spirit, the righteousness of Christ maintains this tie. By fixing our justification in a love that is beyond our own good and evil—above the law—it guards us against all moralistic distortions of the Christian faith. When our pride collapses into the solace of humility, we experience the peace that comes from knowing that Christ is all—our righteousness, our sanctification, our redemption.

Objections to the doctrine of imputation may be justified on the basis that this doctrine can be abused. It easily suffers from second generation deadness. What one generation achieves through struggle and revelation, it tries to pass on without the struggle, as though telling were the same as revealing. What comes to us through involvement with the Spirit cannot be passed on by simply describing the involvement. The Word is inseparable from the Spirit, and the mind is more than intellect. Redemption takes place within the dynamic of relationship, not apart from it. Our correct theological formulations and intellectual comprehension can as easily become a substitute for the relationship of the Spirit as an expression of it. Christ's righteousness is inseparable from Christ. The Christian is not an entity in himself—he exists in relationship to Christ, as branch to vine, as body member to head.

The ease with which formulas and procedures can replace the mystery of the divine-human encounter is illustrated in Olav Hartman's novel, *Holy Masquerade*. The story concerns the skeptic wife of a Swedish clergyman, who systematically attacked each of her husband's defenses for the faith. As the conflict intensified, the wife, Klara, who was barren, began to find faith through a peculiar identification with the Virgin Mary. The Christ she could not accept from her husband Albert's preaching, she seemed to find through an experience that bordered on madness. In a moment of clarity before she died of burns from the mysterious fire in the church tower, she was able with much effort to say, "I have too much in common with Him to deny it. I believe in Him." Although he heard her say this, Albert could not accept it as a genuine confession of faith. Instead he dismissed it as a manifestation of her illness. "It violates all theological principles," he said, "that faith can arise without repentance and guilt."[4]

Even in his creation man is not apart from God. According to the Genesis account his creation in God's image centers in his communion with his Creator. The fall of man marks the rupture of this communion. In his isolation man is estranged not only from God but from his own humanity. It is from this estrangement that Christ redeems us. By his empathic identification with our estrangement, Christ redeemed us from it. In communion with him we reflect his image—his righteousness. Man apart from Christ is man estranged from his own humanity. Faith requires an object. When faith becomes aware of itself as faith it is actually faith in *faith*. When it is faith in Christ, faith-consciousness is overcome by faith's object.

Since faith centers in a relationship, it is also communicated through relationships. The human relationship is either a highway for the Spirit's operation or a roadblock; it is the tangible introduction to the intangible love of God or it is the tangible hindrance. Word and Sacraments do not stand alone, but are committed to the church. As a tangible expression of the fellowship of Christ, the church is the body of Christ. Even as the wages of sin is death (estrangement), so the fruit of redemption is life (communion). Nor is there any discrimination be-

tween man and God in this communion. Each member
of the body is related to Christ in and through his fellow
members, not apart from them.

In pastoral care we utilize this understanding of the
church to communicate God's acceptance. The clinical
observation of the communication of this acceptance
through human relationships elucidates the impossibility
of separating Christ from his saints. We see also why pastoral counseling is more than the giving of advice or the
communication of ideas. The *sina qua non* is the relationship that is established with the pastor. In the rapport of
this relationship the pastor shares his faith not only by
words but by a living experience, through his personal
interest and concern, his acceptance of the unacceptable,
and his attitude of love. In other words, he communicates
the Word in the context of the communion of saints.
Within the dynamic of this relationship the obstacles
created by previous relationships are removed and the
highway is prepared for the Spirit of the Lord.

**V.
Sanctification
Under
God's
Control**

Regardless of what we may learn about sanctification,
the power to sanctify remains with God. Should we even
desire this power, we would be expressing the creature's
lust for the secrets of the Creator—the age-old desire to
be like God. The very nature of sanctification prevents
any possibility on our part of controlling it. One does not
crucify himself, he is crucified. Nor can he resurrect himself being dead. Dying means dying to everything that
would demand anything of ourselves, so that we may
receive again a righteousness that is not our own. This
means in particular that we die to all phoniness in holiness. Nor need we experience any surge of innate goodness
in being resurrected. Rather we are restored to a dominant hope.

The desire to possess the secrets of divinity is not easily

thwarted. In fact, it constitutes the greatest single threat to sanctification. What we cannot possess we tend to simulate. We covet a behavior pattern that appears to be exemplary and proceed to imitate it. Even if this behavior pattern is that of Christ himself, the procedure is doomed from the start. The pattern simply becomes a new law by which we try to live. And as with all conformity to law, it results in a division between the inner and the outer, between the uncontrollable realm of motives, and the controllable realm of observable behavior. Unfortunately we have the power to repress our awareness of this uncontrollable realm, which enables us to possess a tenuous sincerity in our imitation. But it is a static rather than a dynamic sanctification. Conformity to Christ comes not from conforming to a pattern but from the spontaneity of encounter. It is the Gospel and not the Law that transforms. Our sanctification is by faith and not by sight. The New Testament ascribes sainthood to all who are united to Christ. The saint's holiness is his Christ-created status before God as expressed in the baptismal covenant. Therefore it is not the saint who is venerated but the Christ who makes him a saint by faith.

When sainthood is determined by the degree of perceptible sanctification, the saint becomes the object of veneration. He accumulates a surplus of holiness which is stored in a treasury of supererogation and distributed to the less saintly so that equanimity may prevail. Venerating the saints has one of its origins in the period of Roman persecution when those who resisted their persecutors were singled out for adoration in contrast to the defectors. The latter were readmitted into the church only at the cost of serious schism, while the former were exalted in a type of hero-worship.

The elevation of the martyrs to a saintly status may also have been an overcompensation by the rank and file

of Christendom who questioned their own ability to endure persecution. When we are confronted with one who
has made a courageous sacrifice we are smitten with a
vague sort of guilt. Why he and not we? What would we
do if we were in his place? In the absence of answers to
these questions, "praising the hero" has proved a good
substitute. In elevating the holy one, we ourselves feel
holy. Although the situation has changed with modern
travel, the foreign missionary used to be elevated on this
same basis. He represented the ultimate in vocational
sacrifice. Because the majority of Christians are reluctant
to take up their cross, they may feel ill at ease in the
presence of one who seemingly has. All the more reason
to credit him with some sort of superhuman status. If he
is a special category, we are relieved from the painful
process of comparison and can substitute admiration for
imitation. Even the clergyman gets pegged with this
"special class" label. He is considered the religious repre-
sentative and certain restrictions are placed upon him and
his family, from which the layman is excused. His role
is therefore vicarious. However, if the minister is really
the one who equips the laymen to be religious represen-
tatives in their own right, this double standard for laity
and clergy is only a convenient illusion.

Patterns for saintly behavior have varied with the times,
but the cultic elevation of holy ones has been a stable
substitute for holiness. The qualities we admire in others
are usually the qualities we ourselves lack. Envy, said
Kierkegaard, is concealed admiration. Known for qualities we would like to possess, the saint is characterized by
self-control rather than impulsiveness, equanimity rather
than irritability, irenic temperament rather than hot-tem-
pered disposition, dramatic faith rather than doubts and
fears. Regardless of whether the particular pattern of
behavior is based upon the contemplative mode of the

mystics, the moral standards of the puritan, the emotional
vitality of the enthusiasts, or the social concerns of the
ethicist, it is a pattern that usually omits the all too human
reaction of an angry Christ turning over the tables in the
Temple or an irritated Paul wishing castration upon the
Galatians. Because of these superhuman demands upon
our saints, what we consider saintly behavior may be due
as much to weakness, to repression, or to compulsive
neuroses as to the Spirit of God.

Here is where dynamic psychology has been an asset
to the Gospel. It equips us to penetrate the realm of the
inner self, that we may see the ambivalent will behind the
charitable deed, the mixed motivation behind the altruis-
tic act, the negative feelings behind the compulsive smile,
the egocentric reason behind the sacrificial gesture, and
the prohibited hate that alternates with love. We are indebted to the clinical nature of present-day pastoral care
for a fresh insight into the flesh of the saints. Those who
give the impression that they are without original sin
may only be successful in hiding it—even from themselves.
When a man with a wide reputation for his saintly character was being honored by his admirers, he complained
that the plaudits were making it difficult for him to be
humble. The obvious conclusion, of which I am sure he
was unaware, was that he normally thought of himself
as being humble.

Spiritual growth comes about through repentance and
faith. If we take God seriously, we also take sin seriously.
When we walk the way of repentance, our hope is in the
forgiveness of sin. The Spirit who conforms us to Christ
leads us in ever deeper insight into sin. When this happens, we are shocked. We are disappointed in ourselves.
We marvel at the hold that sin has over us. Then out of
this shattering judgment—this crucifixion—we are grasped
by the redeeming presence of the crucified and risen One!

Here is the answer to humanity's predicament. It is Christianity's alternative to repression. In moments of frustration, regret, defeat, and failure in our social, vocational, familial, or even religious pursuits, to be inspired by the Gospel, to affirm with Luther, "I am baptized!"—this is what it means to appeal to a promise, to point to a seal that we are covered by a righteousness that does not fail with our own.

Crucifixion means disappointment: it means experiencing a setback. Otherwise it is not a crucifixion. We are conformed to his image in the fires of dying to the flesh and rising to his likeness. This is not a likeness we can know empirically, for it never moves beyond the sphere of faith. Sanctification is in God's hands. It is by grace and known only to faith. Originating in the foreordaining will of God, sanctification is thus protected from the covetous hands of those who would possess its powers. Sanctification is hidden in the cross and revealed in the resurrection. The cross is overcome, not by our successful bearing of it, but as we begin to realize God's hidden purpose. Our subjective reaction to the resurrection is gratitude. Our subjective reaction to the cross is depression. The leap of faith is expressed by repentance with its hope and committal.

For those whose sanctification lies in imitating Christ, the cross is something other. Fenelon's meditation on Good Friday shows the extreme to which imitation piety can go. The cross for him is a challenge to die with Christ. This emphasis is summed up in his concluding prayer:

> O Savior, let who will sip thy bitter cup; as for me I want to drain it to the lees. I am ready to suffer shame, sorrow, ridicule, and insult from men and inwardly to feel the trial of what may seem to be an abandonment by my heavenly Father. In spite of my shrinking human nature I shall say as Thou hast taught me,

'Father, remove this cup from me; nevertheless, not my will but Thine be done.' These truths are too strong for those who would only half know them and can follow Thee only in the consolations of Tabor. As for me, I should be denying the reality of Thy love if I should draw back.

Come, let us go to Christ. Let us go to Calvary. My soul is sad even unto death; but what does it matter so long as I die pierced with the same nails and on the same Cross as my Savior.[5]

The fact that this is a Good Friday prayer makes it all the more remarkable that there is no reference to the cross as the act of God to redeem his fallen humanity. Instead we see a Christ who leads the way of true piety and inspires us by his example to follow—to accompany him. The efficacy of the atonement lies in its power to inspire others to follow the same example. Do we not have to die even to the desire to die before we can really die? Is there not in Fenelon's prayer the touch of the masochist? Leave it to the flesh to cash in on the act of atonement! How better to render it harmless to itself—to reduce its offense! Anything to avoid hitting that bottom where, beaten to the point of utter defeat, we have no pride left to swallow. Then it is that God can pick up the pieces, put them together, and breathe into us again the spirit of life. We have not beaten ourselves; we have *been* beaten. It is the work of the Holy Spirit.

Obviously something happens to man in his redemption, even though we cannot put our finger on the formula. Job, for example, is a different person after his encounter with God. His whole attitude was changed even though his wretched physical condition was as yet not alleviated. But the difference was not something that Job had accomplished—it was the result of what obviously had happened to him. The atmosphere of dying and

rising is the atmosphere of humility. God's grace is received by faith, and faith opens a whole new dimension
to life. The experience of being forgiven generates a
spirit of forgiveness toward others. Being humble does
not mean being aware of our humility—it means being
aware of our need for grace. Faith and forgiveness exist
in humility; yet humility is not faith, but the result of
faith.

Although something happens in redemption, no formula for this happening exists, and therefore no examples
can be given. Since it is not perceptively perceived, no
identification is possible. God does not permit his revelation to be placed in the categories of science. His Gospel
is received by faith and not by sight. The divine is hidden
in, with, and under the human. It is revealed only to the
faith which grace itself has evoked.

Footnotes

1. Viktor Frankl, *Man's Search for Meaning: An Introduction to Logotherapy*, © 1959, 1962, Viktor E. Frankl (New York: Washington
   Square Press, 1963), p. 59.
2. *Ibid.*, p. 107.
3. *Ibid.*, p. 142.
4. Olav Hartman, *Holy Masquerade* (Grand Rapids, Mich.: Wm. B.
   Eerdmans Publishing Co., 1963), p. 138.
5. *Meditations and Devotions of Fenelon* (London: A. R. Mowbray
   and Co., Ltd., 1954), p. 47.

CHAPTER FOUR

Incarnation and Sacrament

The resurrected life is lived in the world and not re-moved from it. Because creation had gone awry Christ came to redeem it. He identified himself with it in order to save it. So the Christian also is in the world to redeem it. Because like Christ he is not of the world he can change the world. God has resurrected him from the death of sin that he might enjoy the good life that God has created for him. The milieu in which he lives his resurrected life is the sensory, tangible, secular world. As in the creation, so also in the redemption of creation, God looked upon all that he had made, and behold it was good. The identi-fication of God with his creation in the incarnation of Christ has set the pattern for our own involvement in life.

The doctrine of the incarnation has become identified with Athanasius, the church father who so successfully defended it at the Council of Nicea. Athanasius described the incarnation in many ways, of which the following is an example. "At one and the same time—this is the won-der—as Man He was living a human life, and as Word He was sustaining the life of the universe, and as Son He was in constant union with the Father. . . . Just as the sun is not defiled by the contact of its rays with earthly objects, but rather enlightens and purifies them, so He who made the sun is not defiled by being made known in a body, but rather the body is cleansed and quickened by His indwelling."[1]

**I.
Offense
at
Incarnation**

Athanasius' words were not written in the calm of contemplation but under the pressure of battle. The offense of the incarnation was the major problem for Christianity as it came in contact with the dominant religious sentiment of the Greek world. While the church countered this offense successfully in the great creedal battle of the early centuries, it succumbed in the practical problems of sanctification. There was resistance to applying the Gospel to the world of creation—the world of nature. Instead it was applied to the world of spirit in separation from the world of nature. Even in our twentieth century the church has not been fully successful in rising above the religious sentiment of the ancient Greek world.

There is a fundamental difference between the Greek and the Hebrew views of nature. In the Platonic world God was sought beyond nature. In contrast, the God of the Hebrews was actively involved in nature. In harmony with their views each culture had its divergent ideas concerning the communication between God and man. The Hebrews believed that God communicated through events in the world of creation, while the Greeks sought him through their contemplative reason which elevated the seeker above the world of nature.

This difference also led to divergent views of the body-soul relationship. For the Greeks the soul was incarcerated in the body—its prison house—and its fulfillment was in its release from this bondage. For the Hebrews the relationship between body and soul was much less divisible. Consequently, the Greeks had a clearer conception of immortality than the Hebrews, since death emancipated the immortal soul from its corporeal prison. Death for the Hebrews, however, was an enigma, with only a vague conception of a hereafter as a land of shadows. "Where then is my hope?" asks Job. "Who will see my hope? Will it go down to the bars of Sheol? Shall we descend together into the dust?" (Job 17:15-16).

The difference between Greek and Hebrew thought led also to a differing conception of sin. For the Greeks, sin centered in a preference for the sensory world over the spiritual or contemplative world. For the Hebrews, sin centered in idolatry as a spiritual activity that substituted for genuine worship. While idolatrous worship included sensory experience, it was in essence a spiritual activity. Although the cult prostitute added to the appeal of the neighboring religions in Canaan, the judgment upon them was still that of idolatrous *worship*.

Developing out of the Hebrew tradition, the idea of the incarnation involves God in the world of his creation. Jesus attacked the sins of the spirit. "Out of the heart" proceed murders, adulteries, and thefts (Mark 7:21). For Paul sin is also essentially spiritual. The flesh *(sarx)* that lusts against the Spirit includes our bodily appetites, but centers in the perversity of our spirit. This understanding of sin is essential for all sanctification that is genuine. Otherwise a "good spirit" is directed to discipline a "wayward flesh," and such thinking results in a character-trait caricature of sanctification.

The church recognized this rejection of nature as heresy when it appeared in an extreme form. Because the Manichean sect condemned nature as essentially evil, even to the point of dissociating its creation from God, the church condemned it as a denial of the Christian doctrine of creation. Also the docetic heresy was recognized and rejected. As early as in the letters of John, the church was on guard against the cultural tendency to deny the genuine humanity of Christ in favor of an *apparent* humanity. "Every spirit which confesses that Jesus Christ has come in the flesh is of God" (1 John 4:2). This exaltation of the body and of life in the sensory world was an offense to the Greek mind.

But a more subtle rejection of nature penetrated into Christian thinking with comparative ease. We have an example of this penetration in *The Epistle to Diognetus.* In this second-century Christian writing the idea of the incarceration of the soul in the body is assumed as Christian. In attempting to persuade Diognetus of the truth of Christianity the anonymous writer states:

> In a word: what the soul is in the body, that the Christians are in the world. The soul is spread through all the members of the body, and the Christians throughout the cities of the world. The soul dwells in the body, but is not part and parcel of the body; so Christians dwell in the world, but are not part and parcel of the world. . . . The soul is locked up in the body, yet is the very thing that holds the body together; so, too, Christians are shut up in the world as in a prison, yet it is precisely they that hold the world together. . . . The soul, when stinting itself in food and drink, fares the better for it; so, too, Christians, when penalized, show a daily increase in numbers on that account.[2]

According to this viewpoint, man is divided into a good soul consigned to the prison of a very non-spiritual body. The more the soul penalizes the activities of the body, even its eating and drinking, the better it fares. Yet this epistle expressed the common rather than the heretical opinion of the church of that day. Thus we fail to recognize what we supposedly reject simply because it is not apparent in its less extreme forms. If this is the case, the church's rejection of the Greek view may have been primarily a doctrinal necessity, while the feelings involved were more associated with the cultural environment. Even in a later age, a nature lover like Francis of Assisi, who addressed the earth as Mother Earth, addressed his body as Brother Ass. Not until it was too late did he confess that he was too hard on Brother Ass. With this belated change in attitude came also the change to "Brother Body."

When we speak of the incarnation we refer to the birth, life, death, resurrection, and ascension of Christ, even though we focus on his birth. In like manner, when we speak of the sacrifice of Christ we are referring to his birth, life, death, resurrection, and ascension, even though we focus on his death. Even our church calendar shows this differentiation in emphasis. Christmas is the festival of the incarnation, Good Friday commemorates the sacrifice, and Easter is the celebration of the resurrection. In the incarnation we see God continuing and fulfilling the Old Testament pattern of revealing himself through events in the world of creation. It is not surprising that Christological controversies developed early in the life of the church, nor that these focused on intellectual definitions of substance. These controversies preserved the doctrine of the union of the human and divine natures in Christ against the open attacks of those who would make Christ something less than God to preserve his humanity or something other than man to preserve his divinity.

II. From Sacrament to Life

To the Greek mind the natural could not unite with the supernatural. One or the other had to be sacrificed. Even for the orthodox faction the union was difficult, because they too were part of the Greek culture. Athanasius himself is an example in point. Though he was the

chief defender for the full divinity and humanity of
Christ, his theological position did not eliminate his mis-
givings over the world of nature. For Athanasius the incarnation is God's condescension to an inferior world of
nature more than an expression of love for the sinner. In
terms of the Greek dichotomy of body and soul, he con-
ceived of Christ's humanity as his body and his divinity
as his soul—shades of the old idea of the soul incarcerated
in the body. His position raised the question of whether
or not Christ had a *human* soul. Although Athanasius
never denied that Christ had a human soul, his argument
from silence prepared the way for a later follower, Apollinarus, openly to deny it. Again because Apollinarus'
position was obvious and extreme, it was recognized as
heresy.

The controversy over the incarnation extends to the
related doctrine of the Sacrament. Actually the Lord's
Supper continues the idea of the incarnation in that the
earthly elements that are received are identified with the
heavenly. "The cup of blessing which we bless, is it not a
participation in the blood of Christ? The bread which we
break, is it not a participation in the body of Christ?"
(1 Cor. 10:16). When he needed an argument against
the doctrine of transubstantiation in the Lord's Supper,
Luther used the incarnation. Even as no doctrine of
transubstantiation—the changing of the human element
into the divine—is necessary to explain the union of the
divine and the human in the incarnation, so no such
doctrine is necessary to explain the union of the divine
and the human in the Sacrament. As we have the docetic
and the Arian extremes in regard to the incarnation, so
we have the corresponding extremes in pure symbolism
and transubstantiation in regard to the Lord's Supper.

The issue at stake is the relationship of God to nature.
The Sacrament, like the incarnation, is an expression of

this relationship. The celebrants bring bread and wine—elements of nature—to the table. In some sections of the pre-Nicean church each communicant brought his own bread and wine and deposited them on a table at the rear of the church. When the time for the celebration of the Sacrament arrived, the deacons brought these staples of daily sustenance to the altar for the Lord's blessing. In the drama of reenactment the Lord takes, blesses, breaks, and gives. With the food, bread and wine, the believer receives the food, the Body and Blood of Christ.

The eucharistic or thanksgiving prayer that is included in many of the ancient Communion liturgies probably has as its model the *berakhah,* the customary form of blessing or grace at the Passover Kiddush meal. In this passover blessing the participants bless the Lord for the fruits of the earth and for his covenant with the people now gathered before him. In the eucharistic prayer at the Lord's Supper the participants give thanks, not only for creation, but for the Creator himself who is received *with* his creation. Thus creation is "consecrated by the *word of God* and *prayer*" (1 Tim. 4:5). The *Word of God* is the event of redemption—the broken body and the shed blood. The sanctifying *prayer* is the praise and adoration of those who have received. So the Sacrament utilizes the elements from the world of nature as means of grace—as means of receiving God, of evoking thanksgiving, and of sharing with others.

This association of God with his creation extends outward from the Sacrament into life as a whole. For the believer all of life is a means of receiving—it is sacramental. Therefore his whole life becomes a eucharist—a psalm of praise. It is from this vantage point that we can understand the exhortation, "Give thanks in all circumstances; for this is the will of God in Christ Jesus for you" (1 Thess. 5:18). While he was in a Nazi prison cell, Dietrich Bon-

hoeffer received a present from his family for Whitsun-
tide. In his isolated existence this material gift took on
sacramental significance. In acknowledging the gift he
wrote, "Such things give me greater joy than I can say.
Although I am utterly convinced that nothing can break
the bonds between us, I seem to need some outward token
or sign to reassure me. In this way material things become
vehicles of spiritual realities. I suppose it's rather like the
need felt in all religions for sacraments."[3] So also Paul,
writing to the Philippians from his prison cell, thanked
them for a similar gift, not because he was in need of it
as such, but because he was in need of the evidence it
provided of their love. "Not that I complain of want
. . . yet it was kind of you to share my trouble" (Phil.
4:11, 14).

The Christian orientation of the believer's life to the
world of creation is implicit in the doctrine of the Trinity.
The Father's work is associated with creation, and the
Son's work with redemption. But redemption is not apart
from creation; rather it occurs within creation and extends
to the whole of creation.

> For the creation waits with eager longing for the re-
> vealing of the sons of God; for the creation was sub-
> jected to futility, not of its own will, but by the will
> of him who subjected it in hope; because the creation
> itself will be set free from its bondage to decay and
> obtain the glorious liberty of the children of God (Rom.
> 8:19-21).

The Holy Spirit's work is associated with realization.
He internalizes Christ's redemptive work in the life of
the believer. "He will take what is mine and declare it
to you" (John 16:15). He converts the facts of history into
faith. He makes objective history become personal his-

tory, my history. "No one can say 'Jesus is Lord' except
by the Holy Spirit" (1 Cor. 12:3). To accomplish this he
utilizes the means of grace from the world of creation—
the book, the water, the bread and wine, and the human
fellowship. Thus the specific functions of the persons of
the Trinity illustrate the mutuality between nature and
Spirit. It is the redeemed person who realizes this mutuality as he involves himself in the world of creation.

In spite of the emphasis on the union of nature with *III.*
spirit in the Christian kerygma, there have always been *"Spiritualizing"*
those within the church who "spiritualize" this kerygma *Threat*
in the same way the ancient Greeks did. Regardless of
the age in which they appear, these spiritualizers seek the
removal of *means* of grace and *masks* of God in favor of
direct contact. Rising above the "encumbrances" of a
sensory and temporal world, they seek a timeless and
naked encounter with the Divine Spirit. Among the Quie-
tists of the eighteenth century, for example, even the
mental image or mental symbol was discarded as a means
for meditation. Rather than thinking *of God* or even
thinking *about God,* they preferred to "think God." In
coveting the naked God apart from his creation, they
showed their offense at the incarnation.

The Epistle to the Colossians was written to combat an
early form of this spiritualizing tendency. The apostolic
writer desired to make the Word of God fully known so
that the Christians of Colossae might not be taken in by
the specious arguments of an odd sort of Judaistic-Hel-
lenist philosophy which depended upon visions and rejected the physical in behalf of the spiritual. These Colossian spiritualizers were taking others to task over what
they should eat and drink, and like most legalists they
concentrated on "touch not, taste not, handle not." Their

mortification of the body, ritual of angel worship, and their studied cultivation of humility gave the impression of strong spiritual piety.

So far as the Apostle was concerned, however, they were only dealing with shadows. The solid reality is Christ who, as the head, binds and holds the whole body together. He accuses them of devising a religion of this world with their injunctions concerning the elemental spirits—a religion that was of no use in combating the flesh. Christ alone can defeat the flesh, for he alone has primacy over all created things. Openly triumphing over these elementary religious powers through the victory of the cross, he rescued us from the darkness of religious ignorance. The complete being of the Godhead dwells in Christ and through him we too have become complete, for in him are hidden all the riches of wisdom and knowledge. This is God's mystery and the Apostle encourages his readers to recognize it. For we have died with Christ to these elemental spirits through the forgiveness of sin in order that we might be raised with Christ to that higher realm beyond the wisdom of this world. Since the believer is raised above this primitive religion, the Apostle encourages him to put to death what is earthly about him and to put on those qualities which come from above— exhorting him to carry these qualities into every area of life, marriage, family, and vocation—in the sure and certain hope that when Christ who is our life shall appear we also shall appear with him in glory.

In spite of its apparent opposition to carnality, the ascetism of "touch not, taste not, handle not," is simply another form of carnality, in which man has attempted to resolve on a very primitive level the paradox of feeling guilty over tendencies before which he also feels helpless. How then to escape this frustration? The tangible is always easier to control than the intangible. Consequently the outward behavior of the body becomes a scapegoat for the inner workings of the spirit. If the body is the source of evil, we feel more in control than were it the spirit behind the body.

But the conflict is not eliminated by the substitution of body for spirit. Pastoral care offers abundant evidence for this. The use of psychosomatic medicine shows how the body continues to serve as a scapegoat even for the consequences of sin. The bodily symptom is the tangible expression of a conflict that is too threatening to face. In pastoral counseling this conflict may emerge into consciousness to expose the deception of spiritualized religion. The security of the counselee in this situation depends upon his not seeing the connection between the physical symptom and the workings of his spirit. He finds himself in the awkward position of fearing the very help he supposedly desires. The patient acceptance of the pastor, however, may encourage him to cast furtive glances into himself. What he sees may show that despite his rigid controls his self-image has deteriorated. The body cannot be understood apart from the spirit any more than the spirit can be understood apart from the body. Behind the façade of those who judge themselves and others on the basis of "touch not, taste not, handle not," there is often the compensatory indulgence in sexual fantasy or perhaps even a subrosa episode in indulgent behavior. Yet their guilt over these compensations only intensifies their rejection of the body.

Psychiatrist Gotthard Booth believes that the workings of our physical nature are as purposeful as those of our mental or spiritual nature. The soul's relationship to the body is not like Plato's analogy of the chariot driver to the horses because the physical also functions according to purpose and individuality. Rejecting all dualism of body and mind, Booth believes that the two work together in expressing the person. As a physician he interprets disease as an expression of personality and associates specific illnesses with specific personality patterns or needs. The cancer patient, for example, tends to be aggressive and desirous of control, while the tuberculosis patient is inclined to be a dependent person. The cardiac patient tends to be a conformist while the arthritic person is inclined to individualistic self-assertion. Booth sees these illnesses as balancing influences which restrain the natural tendency of the person so that its complement may also develop.[4]

He interprets sexual behavior in a similar way. The youth who is addicted to masturbation is the lonely youth who is making up for his lack of emotionally satisfying relationships by his sexual fantasy. His lack of love is compensated by this expression of loving himself. People who are sexually seductive are usually experiencing a desperate desire for meaningful relationships. "The real need is for emotional, not for genital intercourse."[5]

This displacement of spirit to body turns a person against his own nature. By eliminating all spiritual meaning from bodily appetites and allowing no physical significance to spiritual activities, he makes it impossible to understand his own actions. Because he recognizes no communication between body and spirit, he assumes that none takes place. Consequently he becomes the victim of his own impulsive desires and erratic behavior. Such is the inevitable failure of any dualistic conception of man to bring about self-control. It demands so much of the spirit that repression is the only recourse, and so little of the body that neglect is the inevitable outcome. "True, it has an air of wisdom, with its forced piety, its self-mortification, and its severity to the body; but it is of no use at all in combating sensuality" (Col. 2:23 NEB). Ironically it is the "worldly religion," the Colossian spiritualizing, that rejects the world, and the "religion from above" that accepts it. The key to the difference is the doctrine of redemption.

Spiritualized religion devalues the role of nature in religious experience. God is received in withdrawal from sensory experience or from other than religiously oriented sensory experience. Life in the body is at best religiously inconsequential. In contrast, the incarnation places the created world in a mediatorial position between God and man. This mediatorial position is not simply an abstract inference of the Creator from his creation upon which one could base an ontological argument for the existence of God. Rather it is a mediation which brings about a personal relationship between the Creator and the creature in his own image. God is active in the world of creation, and as we involve ourselves in this world we are involving ourselves with him. Since this world of creation includes people as well as things, and *knowing* as well as *sensing*, involvement with God takes place in the city as well as in the country, in friendship as well as in sensory delight.

But it is possible to miss him—to "worship and serve the creature rather than the Creator." In our natural state we are prone to confuse God's mask with God. When this happens the created things become ends in themselves. We make idols out of them. Nature is a mediator for God's communication only in the relationship of redemption. All of creation must submit to the judgment of the cross. The change that comes about through the death of the distorted ego and the resurrection of the divine image clarifies our vision. The Holy Spirit brings Christ's redemptive work to us in the world of creation so that we can receive him in this creation. Nature and grace are united by Christ and therefore are united in the Christian's experience.

Spiritualizing religion also devalues the role of history.

Since history concerns itself with life in this world, it is only of subsidiary importance. As the Greeks viewed history, it was a series of meaningless cycles. This corresponds to the Greek attitude toward nature. In contrast, the Hebrew view of history sees each day as a fresh and unique opportunity. Although each moment is influenced by the preceding moment, it is not predestined by it. History has a goal. Since God works his purposes through events in time, every moment is potentially open to divine intervention. As we would expect, this view of history is consistent with the Hebrew view of nature, for history takes place in nature. Both are mediums in which God reveals himself, and if revelation occurs in one, it occurs also in the other.

We see this spiritualizing tendency in the extremities of the existentialist emphasis of our day. According to the existentialists, the challenge before us is to face the tragedy of our existence and to affirm ourselves in spite of it. This tends to make everything center, not only upon the present moment, but also upon oneself. The existentialist position is a reaction against a previous overemphasis upon the historical in which the Christian Gospel was almost bereft of any present tense. The historical extreme of older orthodoxy also rejected the significance of history, for although it emphasized a specific epoch of history, it did not extend this significance to the believer's personal history. Jesus was Lord only of sacred history—biblical history. In contrast, the existentialist position in its emphasis on self-affirmation may lose sight of this epoch in the past that makes such self-affirmation possible. In concentrating on the present moment before God, existentialism neglects the historical roots of this moment in redemptive history.

The balance is again in the Sacrament. We bring to the Sacrament the remembrance of him. "This do in re-

membrance of me." Here is appreciation for the past. But
this remembrance of history is joined with an activity in
the present, namely, communion with Christ and his
saints. In both the old and the new covenants, ceremonies
of remembrance play an important role in the religious
life. Besides keeping the historical roots of the covenant
alive through remembrance, these ceremonies keep the
covenant alive by converting the past into a present experience. The Sacraments express the biblical faith that
history and nature together are vehicles for receiving God
in the ongoing drama of redemption.

The spiritualizing attack on the incarnation confronts
us with the question whether the way of sanctification is
in withdrawal from or involvement in the common, everyday life of human existence. We have in the Sacraments
elements of nature—water, bread, wine—which together
with the Word of God serve as means of grace. These
specific means are the channels through which the Gospel of redemption is communicated. But the believer's
communication with God is not confined to his specific
involvement with the means of grace. Rather these serve
as the necessary basis through which God speaks in all of
life. Through these specifically selected forms of nature
the Spirit equips us to receive him in the whole of nature.
This extension of God's communication from the means
of grace to creation as a whole is implicit in the fact that
these special means are inseparable from the social milieu
of the communion of saints. In a limited sense the believer
is also an incarnation—an incarnation of the incarnate
Christ. He takes the fellowship of Christ with him into all
his involvements in life. Luther referred to the Christian
as a "little Christ" to his neighbor. In our day Joseph
Haroutunian suggests that the mental image for the Holy
Spirit be the image of our neighbor in Christ. The church

*IV.
Withdrawal
or
Involvement*

as the communion of saints is the living setting, the context, which undergirds and clothes the Word and Sacraments. As this fellowship reaches out beyond itself, so also the Word and Sacraments extend God's communication into the totality of life experiences.

The only alternative to this position is an intermittent theistic excursion from an otherwise deistic view of life. Such an alternative would erect again the wall of partition between one's religious life and his secular life—a schizophrenia from which Christ came to free us so that he might unite our whole life in him. It would create an artificial gulf between the natural and the supernatural, between the religious life and the common life, and could easily lead to a morbid interest in miracles and a vicarious adoration of anemic brands of saintliness.

But there are those who believe that withdrawal from the common life places a person in a more advantageous position for sanctification. One of the most persuasive of these in our generation is the Roman Catholic apologist Louis Bouyer. Sacrificing the common life for life in a religious order "does not imply any kind of condemnation of the things which it gives up," he maintains, "but simply an absolute preference for 'the one thing necessary.' "[6] The assumption is that life with God is realized more fully apart from the common life. While marriage, for example, can become an individual realization of the love which unites Christ to his church, "it is no less true that many people feel called upon to renounce this genuine but necessarily limited realization of charity in order to devote themselves entirely and immediately to its total realization."[7] While he acknowledges that married couples and ascetics are equally necessary to the church and even concedes that the testimony of Christian couples is necessary to prevent ascetics from making asceticism an end in itself, he goes on to say that their testimony is necessary also to prevent ascetics "from forgetting that they themselves have not renounced love as a whole but simply a limited, imperfectly clarified realization of it in favor of a purer and more immediately boundless one."[8] It is obvious that the more Bouyer tries to maintain the equality of the common life as an alternative to asceticism in the pursuit of sanctification, the more he draws the comparison in a way unfavorable to the common life—namely, that the flesh has less opportunity in the ascetic life. Not that the ascetic "gives up the things of this world in themselves; he only gives up ways of possessing them which carry within themselves the seeds of their own decay."[9]

While we agree that ascetic contemplation is a way of life with God, we contend that it is no higher way than involving ourselves in the common life. But with this Bouyer would disagree. "What distinguishes the monk, the member of a religious order or anyone who takes a particularly ascetic path from the ordinary Christian," he says, "is simply that instead of waiting for the Cross to come to him and force itself on him, he goes to it of his own accord."[10] How can the way of the ascetic be the cross when it bears the status symbol and purgatorial advantages of the higher morality? Since when does one decide beforehand what constitutes the cross for him? While a person may bear his cross in a religious order, it is not because of the religious order. In fact, he may have espoused the ascetic life to avoid the cross. Outer circumstances do not determine what is or is not a sacrifice for Christ. Only inner motivation does this. Even "giving one's body to be burned" is no sacrifice unless the motivation is love.

Bouyer shows how little he understands this point when he says, "The sacrifice must prove its reality by displaying a charity whose universal generosity is really richer and purer than the generosity of a Christian father of a family."[11] A sacrifice can no more prove itself a sacrifice than charity can prove itself to be charity. By means of specific vocations, Catholicism attempts to define maximal and minimal levels of holiness—the reverse of its division of iniquity into maximal and minimal levels of sin.

But Roman Catholics have no corner on asceticism. Protestants have their own varieties of "touch not, taste not, handle not." Neither group, however, can see the value in the specific abstentions of the others. The Roman Catholic may have difficulty in seeing the value of abstention from alcohol, tobacco, and the dance, even as the Protestant may be unable to appreciate an asceticism which abstains from marriage and ownership of property. In fact, the Protestant ascetic would probably censure his Roman Catholic counterpart for participating in alcoholic beverages and condemn the Roman Catholic Church for sponsoring parish dances. Since it allows for only one level of religious involvement, the Protestant form of asceticism is more arbitrary than the Roman Catholic form. Either the believer adopts the recommended abstentions or he is not genuinely converted.

Protestants also have their own variety of the higher morality in the status given to professional church workers. The mental image the laity has of foreign missionaries, deaconesses, and even pastors often elevates them above the earthly problems of the ordinary layman. These professional churchmen have responded to the call for greater sacrifice and consecration, and therefore must to some extent be removed from the life of normal human aspirations and passions. They belong to the "third sex" if for no other reason than their choice of a religious profession. "It's hard for me to think of ministers as people," said one honest teenager. Is there any wonder, then, that he would discount the possibility that he should study for the ministry?

But the redeeming factor is that this Protestant counterpart to Roman Catholic ascetism is not fixed in an established doctrine. Therefore there is always the opportunity for purging. On the other hand, the Roman Catholic higher morality is fixed in dogma and is therefore no longer even subject to question. Both forms, however, divert attention from the flesh as the egocentric motivator even for the "good." In pastoral counseling these outward supports give way to the disturbing realm of motives and ambivalences and even to recollections of secret aberrations.

As an example, there was the man who could have merited the sobriquet of "Helpful Henry." He was continually cheerful and outgoing, even with his family—being especially solicitous toward his wife. He sought pastoral counseling because his inner life did not possess the equanimity that his countenance indicated. The man had been having attacks of anxiety which were associated with a recurring dream in which he would kill his wife—at first accidentally but later deliberately. Now the thought of such a deed would enter his mind while awake—and terrify him.

Man: I am afraid I might do it—although it's the last thing in the world I would want to do.

Pastor: You have no antagonism toward your wife.

Man: Heavens no! In fact, she says I'm an ideal husband. I try to be as helpful as I can to her.

Pastor: I'm not referring to your actions, but to your feelings. Have you never felt angry toward your wife even though you didn't show it?

Man: I—I don't know what to say. I never let myself feel angry. It doesn't do any good to be angry —it just causes trouble.

Pastor: Yet you have these very violent thoughts.

Man: Yes—doesn't make sense, does it!

Pastor: It might if as you say being angry causes trouble.

Man: How it that?

Pastor: This may be the trouble it's causing *you*.

This man feared his own potential for being destructive because he could not countenance the normal emotion of anger. Instead he became even more concerned with pleasing his wife. Yet he could not afford to be spontaneous. His dreams and obsessions were nature's way of trying to right the imbalance. The more rigid the outer role, the more pressure for a secretive indulgence.

There is no life situation in which it is easy to live the Christian life. The potential is primarily within ourselves. There are situations that do not present the apparent temptations that may be found elsewhere. But the lack of obvious temptations may open the door for a greater temptation. The very ease offered by a protective environment may cause us to lower our guard so that we are taken captive by the adversary without even being aware of it. Where is there a more protected environment than the campus of a theological seminary? Yet every student knows the insidious temptations that exist in such a community. In monologuing with those of his own kind, he may become shallow because he is safe. The environment with the more obvious temptations to the flesh may also bring about more frequent crucifixions of the flesh. Paul's "more excellent way" of love does not depend on preferential environments.

In withdrawal we are seeking protection. Sometimes this is necessary. Yet it is not the main direction for sanctification. The ultimate answer to abuse is not disuse but use. Those who continue to withdraw are more concerned with protection than growth. They are safeguarding their virtue by not putting it to the test. The Christian is called upon to live for Christ and not for his own salvation. He is called upon to lose his life and not to save it. If one loses to find, he is not really losing. Though others may see and praise our sacrifice, our guilt remains, for we know that God alone knows our motives.

The need of some people to depreciate a compliment is an example of this guilty self-awareness. Some of this depreciation is due to the normal "Christian" desires to appear humble; yet without realizing it, one loses all humility by such an obvious play for it. Some have been brought up to think of any honest assertion of their worth as pride and therefore sinful, and so they overcompensate for such tendencies by becoming self-depreciative. One may also depreciate a compliment, however, because he knows all too well that his inner attitude does not correspond to his outer accomplishment—knowledge of which the complimenter is obviously unaware. He cannot endure praise because he knows the praiser does not know what *he* himself knows; so he sabotages the compliment. If the praise persists, he may be driven to sabotage also the *basis* for the compliment—to deliberately wreck his reputation. The "good girl," for example, may want to "let go" and be bad because she has never believed she *was* good and felt guilty over the dishonest label. We are reminded of Jesus' words, "One there is who is good" (Matt. 19:17).

Ascetic withdrawal may be a flight from the challenges and demands of maturity. The sacrifices of family living, the responsibilities for making decisions, and the challenges of economic stewardship constitute a continuous and difficult demand upon our love. And because of these demands we are continuously exposed to failure—and hence crucifixion. In withdrawal we are spared the judgment. But it is through judgment that we grow. As redeemed persons we take our redemption into life rather than retreat from it. Since the flesh is put to death through the failures we experience in our own resources, these experiences of involvement in life such as marriage and the family may serve the cause of such mortification very well. God comes to us, not apart from his creation, but in, with and under it. The illusion that God is found apart from the common life is similar to the illusion that God can be loved apart from man or that Christ can be separated from his saints.

Redemption enters creation through the redeemed person. It is not eros or mammon that is redeemed but the person who has eros and who deals with mammon. The integration with life takes place within the person. To withdraw from the common life for the sake of our sanctification contradicts the obvious implications of the incarnation and the sacrament.

Religion is not simply one activity among others, but rather a new orientation that affects all of life. The Gospel is more than a religion—it is a way of life (Acts 9:2; 22:4). Because of his orientation to life, the Christian receives most fully when he involves himself in life at its most demanding edge. The same is true in his human relationships. It is in our uninterrupted living together that we develop the strongest ties of devotion. Although this continuous experience has its negative as well as its positive moments, close relationships grow out of negative experiences also. How better to learn than to let our ways be put to the test. Granted that it is wise at times for people to get away from each other, these withdrawals may also be escapes. When we are unable to withdraw from people simply because we are wearied of them, we face new demands upon our relationships that may strengthen our own development as well as our ties with others. The choice is between comfort and challenge, between safety and adventure, between the fear of failure and the courage to risk the attempt.

Since the conflict between those who would unite nature and spirit and those who would separate them centers on the role of the physical and the material in the religious life, their respective ideas about sanctification conflict in this same area. Those who separate nature and spirit lean toward ascetic self-denial, and those who unite them, to receiving the common life with thanksgiving. Does the way of sanctification lie in the ascetic rigor of abstaining or in the eucharistic emphasis of enjoying? Does ascetic self-denial such as fasting belong in the new covenant or has eucharistic receiving taken its place?

Although Jesus fasted forty days, he was not an ascetic. In fact, he was compared unfavorably to John the Baptist by some of his contemporaries for this reason. The very idea of his incarnation implies his participation in the common life. In Mark's Gospel it is stated that he declared all foods clean, that is, he removed even the old covenant taboos concerning certain meats. We see this full participation also in the dream of Peter in which he refused the platter of unclean meats and was admonished by the Lord, "What God has cleansed, you must not call common" (Acts 10:15). Jesus also undermined the contemporary use of fasting as a way of sanctification when he made it a hidden activity. "But when you fast, anoint your head and wash your face, that your fasting may not be seen by men but by your Father who is in secret" (Matt. 6:17-18). What value was there now in fasting when part of the reward was to "appear unto men to fast"? In addition he defended his disciples against the criticism that they did not fast. "Can the wedding guests mourn as long as the bridegroom is with them? . . . And no one puts a piece of unshrunk cloth on an old garment" (Matt. 9:15-16).

Paul extended the principle of the eucharistic reception of creation even to the controversial subject of eating meat that had been offered to idols. Some Christians felt it was wrong to eat such meat since it had been defiled by its previous use in the idol temples. But Paul said, "If I partake with thankfulness, why am I denounced because of that for which I give thanks?" (1 Cor. 10:30).

On the other hand, the apostolic church fasted. Fasting preceded and followed a very important decision at the congregation in Antioch.

> Now in the church at Antioch there were prophets and teachers, Barnabas, Symeon who was called Niger, Lucius of Cyrene, Manaen a member of the court of Herod the tetrarch, and Saul. While they were worshiping the Lord and fasting, the Holy Spirit said, "Set apart for me Barnabas and Saul for the work to which I have called them." Then after fasting and praying they laid their hands on them and sent them off (Acts 13:1-3).

If fasting can help promote decisions such as this, perhaps we ought to advocate it for the churches of today. Fasting also played a role in the lives of the congregations that were established by this first missionary team. In relating their missionary procedure, the Book of. Acts says, "And when they had appointed elders for them in every church, with prayer and fasting, they committed them to the Lord in whom they believed" (Acts 14:23).

In Paul's first letter to his Corinthian congregation we have a clue to the role of fasting in the new covenant. Addressing himself to the conduct of husband and wife toward each other, the Apostle says, "Do not refuse one another except perhaps by agreement for a season, that you may devote yourselves to prayer; but then come together again, lest Satan tempt you through lack of self-control" (1 Cor. 7:5). According to this directive, the purpose of withdrawal from the common life—in this instance the sex relationship in marriage—is not because of any inadequacy in the common life to quicken the spirit, but to devote—to give full attention without distraction—to prayer. Significant of the development of the early church, later manuscripts added the words "and fasting." Yet this marital abstinence *is* fasting. And the necessary precaution for such fasting is to return to the norm of the common life without undue delay.

But even if the common life rather than fasting from the common life is the norm, is the common life in itself a distraction to the spiritual life? Is abstention from it— even if only for a season—an assist to spiritual concentration? *Means* always carry the danger of becoming *ends*. The word idol, for example, is derived from the Greek word "to see." We can so focus our attention on the sensory that we fail to see beyond it. Even the means of grace are not exempt from this danger. The elements of the Lord's Supper may be venerated in themselves, and the Holy Book may be subtly substituted for the Holy Spirit.

If this tendency to distort *means* into *ends* can happen to the means of grace, how much more can it happen to nature as a whole? We are well aware of this possibility in our own age. Whenever there is an emphasis on asceticism in one generation, the succeeding generation usually reacts in opposition. The pendulum swing now is in the direction of involvement in nature as an end in itself. Once we remove involvement from the judgment of the law, we go to the extreme of self-indulgence, as though the only alternative to the rejection of nature is nature worship. Once the restraints are removed, the object of restraint becomes elevated to the *summum bonum*.

Since the law gives nothing, but only restrains, the victims of legalism are often in desperate need of receiving. In their state of deficiency they may grasp in-

discriminately for things to satisfy their emptiness—
whether it be food, alcohol, sex, or money. In the pastoral
care of such people we recognize these biological and
material fixations as symptoms of a spiritual deficiency.
Something vital is missing from their personal development, and sexual agitation and material greed are compensations for this deficiency. There has been no Gospel
to replace the legal restraints and no fellowship to nurture
their emotionally isolated spirits. Lacking a positive sense
of meaning to replace the discarded negative sense, they
have turned to immediate and tangible substitutes that
are gratifying to our acquisitive or sexual impulses. Sex is
a leading substitute for relationships because it is the
most intimate expression of relationship. Since meaning
comes through relationships, sex then becomes an immediate compensation for the lack of meaning. The acqui-
sition of wealth symbolizes power over others, and therefore it is another substitute for relationship. When sex
becomes the *be-all* of life, as it is threatening to become
in our culture, it is the symptom of a very empty and
estranged society. It is hard for us to realize that the
"oversexed" are usually frigid persons. The overcompensation shows where the deficiency lies.

Often such persons realize their lack and look to an environmental change for their answer. Some may think that
only by entering the ministry can meaning be found. Others look to marriage as the panacea. Trusting in a change
of environment is a hazardous risk, since our anticipations
are often unrealistic. Dreams about marriage do not en-
vision the difficult problems ahead for those already
deficient in positive relationships. Nor do anticipations of
life in a religious profession foresee the endless demands
of a tyrannical conscience. We expect more from these
environmental changes than they can give or are even
meant to give. Because our needs are extreme, our de-

mands are insatiable and our prospects are dim. As a medium for self-expression, our environment can assist us but does not substitute for us. Neither marriage nor a religious office is primarily a way of receiving. But when we come to terms with our needs at the deeper level of our fellowship with Christ and his church, we can enter into our environmental changes more optimistically.

Although nature is sacramental in significance, it is also transitory. In spite of our reconciliation with our material world, we do not seek the continuing city here. At the end of nature there is death and decay. We seek the city which is yet to come. This is the eternal dimension in the Christian approach by which all must be evaluated. So long as we look at life from the perspective of eternity we shall be prevented from making idols out of transitory things, and be spared the disillusionment that inevitably overtakes those who seek their continuing city here. Neither marriage, nor career, nor business success, nor social status can substitute for the "one thing needful" in giving satisfaction to life. In the midst of our enjoyment of nature we take the leap of faith to God. "This too shall pass," but he abides forever. Creation serves as a means for receiving God with thanksgiving and not as an end that can substitute for him. What Luther says about the petition for daily bread can be applied to all of God's creation.

> God gives daily bread, even without our prayer, to all people, though sinful, but we ask in this prayer that he will help us to realize this and to receive our daily bread with thanks.[12]

Perhaps it was the degeneration of the mediatorial significance of daily bread that led to the dissociation of the Lord's Supper from its original setting in the love feast. At the conclusion of the fellowship meal, called the *agape*, the Sacrament was celebrated. We have evidence of the degeneration of this custom already in Paul's First Letter to the Corinthians when the Apostle chastises the congregation for turning the sacramental love feast into a gluttonous brawl. Gradually the love feast disappeared. Michael Ramsey, the archbishop of Canterbury, concludes that "the Eucharist had to be set apart from common meals in an awe and mystery whereas its nearness to common life was to be realized more deeply."[13]

Is there a place for fasting in the way of sanctification? The answer is *yes* if our purpose is to concentrate on communion with God. The answer is *no* if our purpose would stem from a negative view of nature in sanctification. The new covenant regulation for fasting is that it be followed by receiving the common life with thanksgiving. Nor is there any question even in the old covenant concept of fasting about nature's mediating role in the spiritual life. Yet in both covenants there is the recognition that we may have to withdraw from the common life on occasion in order to keep our perspective of the common life pure, that is, to keep the role of nature as a means of evoking thanksgiving to God from becoming an end in itself.

Redemption takes place in creation. Otherwise it would have no relevance to human existence. If redemption centers in creation, the cross is the sign of judgment. Since man has misused God's creation by worshiping it, he is in need of redemption. As the manifestation of this redemption, sanctification is focused on receiving the common life with thanksgiving. The matter is aptly put by C. H. Dodd: "This world of things, persons, and events can never forfeit, because of human sin, its one title to reality —namely its fitness to mediate the call of God to man. For it has once been the field upon which the great encounter was fought to a decision, and it bears the mark of the encounter forever."[14]

Footnotes

1. *St. Athanasius on the Incarnation* (London: Mowbray, 1953), pp. 45-46.
2. "The Epistle to Diognetus," *Ancient Christian Writers,* Vol. VI (London: Longmans, Green & Co., 1948), pp. 139-40. Published in U.S.A. by Newman Press, Westminster, Md.
3. Dietrich Bonhoeffer, *Prisoner for God* (New York: Macmillan, 1953), pp. 42-43.
4. See Booth's Introduction to *The Voice of Illness* by Aarne Siirala (Philadelphia: Fortress Press, 1964).
5. Gotthard Booth, "Masturbation," *Pastoral Psychology,* November, 1954, p. 16.
6. Louis Bouyer, *Christian Initiation* (London: Burns and Oates, 1960), p. 141.
7. *Ibid.,* p. 143.
8. *Ibid.,* p. 144.
9. *Ibid.,* p. 142.
10. *Ibid.,* p. 139.
11. *Ibid.,* p. 145.
12. Luther's Small Catechism in Contemporary English.
13. Arthur M. Ramsey, *The Gospel and the Catholic Church* (London: Longmans, Green & Co., 1956), p. 108.
14. C. H. Dodd, *The Apostolic Preaching and Its Developments* (London: Hodder and Stoughton, 1956), p. 96.

CHAPTER FIVE

Christian Experience or Natural Experience

The fact that the Christian life takes place in the common life has always made it difficult to set up any list of characteristics by which the Christian can be perceptibly distinguished from the non-Christian. Being "in the body" we are dependent upon sensory perception, and our difficulty in distinguishing the Christian in this perceptual manner has been a source of continuous frustration to the church. In fact, withdrawing from the common life in monastic retreat has an appeal for this very reason —in withdrawing one is making a distinction which is obviously perceptible.

I.
Describing the Difference

The church, however, has accepted its predicament from the beginning. We can see this in the early Epistle to Diognetus. Says the Epistle, "Christians are not distinguished from the rest of mankind by either country, speech, or customs; the fact is, they nowhere settle in cities of their own; they use no peculiar language; they cultivate no eccentric mode of life."[1] In other words, the Christian, like anybody else in our culture, gets up in the morning, shaves, eats his breakfast, goes to work, enjoys some of it, watches the clock, returns to his home, joins with at least some of the family for the evening meal, reads the newspaper, watches television, grows sleepy, goes to bed.

The fact that we have difficulty in describing the difference does not mean that no difference exists. Again from the Epistle to Diognetus: "Yet while they [the Christians] dwell in both Greek and non-Greek cities, as each one's lot was cast, and conform to the customs of the country in dress, food, and mode of life in general, the whole tenor or their way of living stamps it as worthy of admiration and admittedly extraordinary."[2] In other words, the difference lies not in doing different activities, but in the "tenor" in which these activities are done.

Actually the ancient apologist has not helped us much. We are now left with the problem of describing this "tenor" in a way that would distinguish it from that of the non-Christian. In our many attempts to do this we have been misleading and unreal—in fact, dishonest. Our "Christian" motion pictures and "Christian" fiction are illustrations in point. Since actions alone are not distinctive, we are constrained to show the "Christian" difference in sententious sentences, dramatic speech inflection, or in some other artificial way. The result is not only maudlin and overly sentimental—it is false. Personality is oversimplified; people are one-dimensional. Lacking is the complex, flesh-and-blood, perversely idealistic organism we call man. Consequently the viewer or reader finds it difficult to apply the presentation to his own confused and complicated existence.

One of our frequent escapes from this difficulty to distinguish is to settle for special religious vocations. Here we can picture the "difference." The result has been a spiritual glamorization of first-century martyrdom, of monastic, missionary, and clerical life. Although these special vocations are good frames within which to picture a difference, they may also serve to show up the lack of luster and Christian significance in our ordinary life and in our common occupations.

Are we confronted with an impossibility in presenting a Christian type by which we can picture the Gospel's unique effect? Unfortunately the so-called characteristics of a Christian may also be derived from other sources. If we point to a peaceful and affectionate family life as an example of what Christianity can accomplish, we have to recognize that human nature at its best can produce this also. And if we indicate that the opposite—a disturbed family life—is the result of human nature at its worst, we have to recognize that it may also be a product of the Gospel's divisive influence. Did not Jesus say that he had come not to bring peace but a sword—to set the members of a family in opposition to one another?

What about a strong and disciplined character? May this not result from Christian influence? Here again we have to admit that human nature at its best can produce this quality also. The ancient Greeks were noted for their development of strong and disciplined characters. Nor is an undisciplined and disintegrated character the result only of human nature at its worst. It may also be attributed to the work of the Holy Spirit to undermine one's faith in the sufficiency of his own resources so that he may trust instead in the salvation of God. While such disintegration is a transitional stage in God's economy, one does not always resolve all of his transitional stages.

As Kierkegaard has pointed out, it is one's misfortune not to have the crucifixion experience, and yet it is the most dangerous experience of all. The risk is that there is nothing automatic about its outcome. Human experience always contains the element of the unpredictable. For some the transitional disintegration has meant mental illness. Such was the case with Anton Boissen, the pioneer of the clinical pastoral education movement. It was through his own illness that Boissen developed the insight into mental illness as a crisis in which one struggles for a new and more meaningful existence. For others the *down* experience has meant suicide. There is no assurance either that any of us will live through our transitional experience, since accident and illness are always possibilities. Besides, life itself is one continuous transition stage which is never fully resolved. We are always in the process of movement —of becoming—of passing through one perspective or stage of development to another.

Another Christian attribute is self-sacrifice. Jesus said, "He who loses his life for my sake will find it." But self-sacrifice may also be a mark of atheistic Communism. The devoted Communist may sacrifice his own life—say in battle—for the greater cause of his idolatrous ism. Since God's enemies are not necessarily cowards, they also may be adversity conquerors. Some who are evil may also be brave. A pagan may show more courage in the face of death than a Christian. Looking back upon his frustration as a young pastor to the dying, Reinhold Niebuhr confessed, "While my own simple idealism would have scarcely been equal to the test of facing the ultimate issue, I find myself deeply disturbed by the fact that faith was evidently of so little account in the final test."[3]

II. Similarity in Psychological Behavior

Unfortunately the difference is hard to distinguish even if we penetrate beneath externalities to the inner life. Luther's quarrel with the scholastics was over this very issue. In contrast to their position that a difference exists in the nature of our sinfulness before and after

Baptism, Luther contended that sin remains the same in quality after Baptism as before. The flesh never changes. It can neither be converted nor mitigated; it can only be crucified. The flesh in the Christian is precisely the same flesh that is in the non-Christian. For this reason the Christian can empathize with sinners of all varieties. The understanding that is needed to help another is ours by virtue of our humanity. "There but for the grace of God go I," is no mere pious expression. The flesh is the same before grace as after grace, although in grace it is potentially recessive in character while outside of grace it is potentially dominant.

So there is a difference, but it is not any qualitative difference in our sinful nature. In proportion to his honesty with himself the Christian is aware of the same devious resistance to trusting and listening to the Word of God which seems to threaten him as he normally associates with the pagan. He finds in himself the same perverse will to brood, to panic, to fret, to resent, and to desire retaliation. These are the evidences of an undercurrent of revolt—of a resistance to let God be God—that we would expect to find in the unbeliever. The "flesh" is of the same quality in all of us and is activated in its resistance to God by the very overtures of God's Spirit. The enigmatic idea that God hardens the sinner's heart may simply mean that he will not leave us alone. Rather he is continually approaching us, and this arouses the flesh to resistance. The overtures of God in his goodness influence the resistant to become more resistant, even as they influence the believer to become more of a believer.

Like his unbelieving neighbor, the Christian is consistently profaning the sacred. The difference between the church as a social organization and other social organizations such as service clubs is at times difficult to discern. When we involve ourselves in the organizations of the church, it may be "faith" rather than "sight" that prevents us from becoming disillusioned. The same pettiness and egotism that one discovers in secular organizations are apparent in church organizations, whether it be the women's guild, the minister's fraternal, or the theological seminary. Here we find people who after a fashion have associated themselves with the cause of Christ, but who can become more concerned about the slight to their egos than about anything else. In the administrative structure of the denomination we discover the same sort of machinery we would find in a business corporation, perhaps even the same abuse of power, and even the same rejection of those who oppose the system.

Even the idyllic picture of the group life of the early church had its disillusioning side. Despite our continuous search to recover the lost radiance of this fellowship, there were some features of it that were better to remain lost. Even from the sketchy accounts that we have, we know of Ananias and Sapphira who cheated the common treasury, and about the dissension between the Hellenist and the Hebrew widows over supposed discrimination in the distribution of the common treasury. Even leaders like Paul and Barnabas were so divided in their attitude toward Mark that they could find no solution to their sharp dissension but that each should go his separate way.

Yet these difficulties in the Hebrew church were mild compared to those of the Gentile churches then and in the generations following. The Corinthian congregation was divided by factions. At the celebration of the Lord's Supper the strife between the *haves* and the *have-nots* was such a scandal that it brought a severe rebuke from Paul. Even in his happy letter to the Philippians Paul exhorted certain women of the congregation to reconcile their differences. As the church entered the period of episcopal rivalries and doctrinal disputes, it is even dif-

ficult for us in our awareness of our own intra-church
strife to imagine how Christians could be so unchristian
to each other.

So far as any empirical observation is concerned, psychological reactions provide no evidence of one's theological position, his relationship with God, or his conflict
with the devil. A London striptease artist at one of the
flourishing noon hour clubs of that city was asked by a
reporter concerning her reactions to her work. She stated
that she enjoyed the attendance of the local rugger team
much more than the average business clientele because
the athletes gave a more robust sign of approval to her
art than the rather restrained British businessmen, thus
providing her a greater sense of accomplishment and appreciation. Would a psychological description of her reaction differ appreciably from the reaction of a clergyman
to his congregation's appreciation of his sermon? Only
one's value judgment of the two professions would predispose him to assume a difference in the *psychological*
reactions. In either case the individual projects himself
into his art or his work and becomes either elated or
deflated, depending upon whether the reaction of those
to whom he is directing his efforts is negative or positive.

This example was deliberately chosen because of its
apparent incongruity. To compare a striptease artist to a
clergyman is offensive—poor taste to say the least. Yet
it is precisely this disparity that exists between professions
that makes the minister so depressed when the *similarity*
"hits home." "Is my egocentricity any different because I
serve the church, than the egocentricity of the enterpris-
ing salesman for General Motors?" he asks in one of those
moments of awful insight. In his spoof on the ministry
Charles Merrill Smith advises the young cleric, "So long
as your congregation is enthusiastic about you as a
preacher . . . your reputation as a superior pulpit man

will get around, and better paying churches will be after you."[4] The minister discovers that his *flesh* is about the same as the flesh in anybody else. Though the desires of the Spirit are against the flesh, they do not eliminate it. Nor do they dilute its absolute opposition to God.

Even the psychological dynamic of guilt is not specifically religious. Guilt is a psychic tension created by the difference between the way one perceives that he is and the way he believes he should be. While the Christian views this tension in terms of conscience, the psychiatrist sees it as a factor in mental health. It occurs alike in the "natural" and the "spiritual" man. From the Christian point of view, this guilt is largely distorted in the "natural" man, while the guilt of the Christian also is distorted in part. Like that of any other person, his experience of guilt and depression is closely associated with the lack of appreciation from specific individuals. The difference between his conscience and Freud's super-ego may be empirically indiscernible. Psychologically speaking, guilt is guilt regardless of what causes it.

In the field of psychotherapy there is a growing attack upon the traditional approach to guilt because it minimizes the moral context. The response to this attack shows that many were waiting for someone to challenge the dominating Freudian thought. Guilt is *real*, say these insurgents, and not just a neurotic feeling. Yet no one, including Freud, ever denied that guilt was real or that a person may really be guilty. Guilt can be distorted, neurotic, and immature, but it is no less real, and the person is no less guilty. In neurotic guilt a person feels guilty about the wrong offenses, but is guilty nevertheless, as would be evident were the real issues faced. Those who contrast *real* with *neurotic* seem to believe that real means inerrant—that a person's guilt is always commensurate with his offense. This position is subject to question. Real guilt can be erroneous in its context. It can attach itself to a less threatening context and thus become incommensurate with the offense.

We feel guilty about the wrong offenses because the tension is then easier to bear. The procedure is ancient. Adam said he was hiding from God because he felt guilty over being naked, when the real reason for his guilt was that he had eaten of the forbidden fruit. The challenge in therapy is to stimulate a person's guilt to mature, that is, to identify with a realistic context. It is even conceivable that the person may come to the conclusion that his guilt is a hangover from a past with which he no longer wishes to identify himself. In such a case he may decide that the only guilt he should have is guilt over his guilt. In other words, God is sovereign even over conscience, and one may defy the automatic guilt in the name of Christ as an evidence of his growing maturity.

Although it is sometimes asserted that Christ's atonement puts an end to guilt for the believer, it actually does not. Rather through its influence upon the believer, guilt is converted from a destructive into a constructive tension, and as such is a necessary stimulus rather than an obstacle to self-improvement. Yet, if we tried to describe this change *psychologically*, we might discover that a secular psychiatrist had achieved the same descriptive results with his patient. In other words, there is nothing unique *empirically* about *Christian* guilt.

This frustration in describing a difference between the Christian and the non-Christian either in his outer behavior or in his inner dynamics does not mean that Christianity makes no difference. Rather it illustrates the identification of all of us with the human family, and Christianity does not remove us from this identification. The communion of saints is something in which to believe, not necessarily to perceive. As Calvin put it, we say we *believe* in the communion of saints because "it is often impossible to discover any difference between the children of God and the ungodly, between his peculiar flock and wild beasts."[5]

Even if our Christianity does not remove us from the common lot of human experience, this very identification with the human family has a decided effect upon our Christianity. As human beings we desire the approval of others. Whatever tangible evidence we receive of this approval indicates that our efforts are successful. But signs of success are also interpreted as signs of divine favor. They are testimonies to the fact that "the Lord is with us." By this same token signs of failure are readily interpreted as signs of God's disfavor. This is not merely a primitive level of religious reasoning. By nature we seek for signs. Out of the struggle with adversity the Christian may adapt to his disappointment. He may even grow to "extol reality." But the very fact that he learns to do this in one specific incident may have little carry-over to the next disappointment that he faces. The despair of the saints is that they seem unable to profit from past experience when they meet unexpected frustration or disappointment. Spiritual growth therefore is not comparable to physical growth which is a gradual, lineal, and observable enlargement. Rather, spiritual growth is characterized by a series of new starts. Yet the fact that spiritual growth is unobservable or unempirical does not mean that it is not taking place. This is where faith becomes the evidence of things not seen.

III. Life in the World

Our life with God is closely associated with our life with people. Belief in God is much more "natural" when our needs in human relationships are being met than when they are not. An exchange student studying theology in a foreign country found himself slipping deeper and deeper into despair. His contacts with his fellow students had deteriorated, and his confidence in himself was gone. Sitting alone night after night in his rooming house, he began to think that nobody cared whether he lived or died. Ashamed to return home a failure and overcome with depression in his present environment, he began to be plagued with thoughts of self-destruction. As a desperate measure to call attention to his plight, he attempted suicide. This brought his plight to the attention of his faculty advisor who then arranged for him to move into the dormitory and encouraged other students to visit him, particularly in the evenings. After a few weeks of this care and concern the student felt much better. But now that his depression was lifting, he had a theological problem. If feeling uncared-for and forsaken by people was a cause of his despair and the restoration of his ties with people restored also his faith in God— where or what is God? Is he the same as people?

The need for a response from people is natural. When it is not forthcoming, our feeling tone is negative. Faith and negative feelings are not consciously compatible. What is the role of God here? Is he the victim of a projection? Do we feel that God feels about us somewhat as others do? Or is he the consoler when all others forsake us? Or do we doubt his existence altogether at such a time? When a friend turns cold—when we feel left out and forgotten—we may experience all the emotional dynamics of a religious crisis.

IV.
Baptism
of the
Common

Since the Christian shares in the experiences of the human family his distinctly Christian experience is a sanctification of that which is common. In the catacombs of Rome there is an ancient slab with a Christian inscription. However, as one observes more closely he can perceive under the Christian inscription an older pagan inscription. The same slab had been used by both groups. One of the distinguishing marks of the Christian culture in the early centuries was the highly disciplined monastic system founded by Saint Basil. Actually Basil had taken over the disciplined patterns of Greek philosophy and worked them into a Christian setting. It was the same system. The tune "Innsbruck," to which Paul Gerhardt's hymn "Now rest beneath the shadows" is sung, was originally a drinking song in the local pubs. It was the same tune. Whatever uniqueness the word "Christian" may imply centers in a medium of expression which is not unique. It is a "baptism" of human ways—of natural experience.

We can illustrate this in three functions which have strong religious overtones. The first is the creative ingenuity of inspiration. Despite its use in religious experience, inspiration is a distinctly human capacity. Poets, musicians, inventors, and "idea-men" all depend upon inspiration for their function. Its uniqueness in religious experience is its God-relatedness. In other words, God uses this human quality to communicate with man. A second and related function is the inner light of mysticism. There are non-religious or profane mystics as well as religious mystics. Aldous Huxley produced what he interpreted as a mystical experience with the drug peyote. The uniqueness of religious mysticism is simply in the religious use of mysticism and not in mysticism itself. The possession of clairvoyant and telepathic powers has been associated with religious or even prophetic activity. Today they are recognized as extra-sensory perceptions that some possess and others do not. Although God may use these extra-sensory abilities to carry out his purposes— as he may have done with some of the prophets of Israel —the abilities themselves are natural abilities even though disproportionately distributed.

A third function is associated with the achievement of wisdom. For the religiously minded, wisdom comes through the response of the believer to what God is teaching him in the events of the day. Because of what God has revealed to him in a particular situation, the believer is prepared to meet similar situations more wisely. Despite its religious interpretation, this way of achieving wisdom is what the secular man calls learning from experience. It is the value he receives in reflecting upon history, whether the history of the state, the church, or the self. Its only uniqueness in religious experience is in the concept of God as the teacher.

This reference to the study of history is an example of the role of human learning in Christian experience. Data from these studies expand our understanding of life. Life in this world is not separated from life with God. The understanding, knowledge, and insight that come from the sciences can be used by God in his sanctifying work. They become "baptized" when they are integrated into the larger perspective of God's providence. In the sanctification of the common, two such radically different media as the word of man and the Word of God find their unity, not in some abstract notion in the realm of ideas, but within the dimensions of time and space in our everyday life. God reconciled the world unto himself in the midst of history. The Christ through whom he accomplished his reconciliation remains in our midst by his Spirit.

V.
The
Perspective
of
Faith

Not only does life in the world affect our life with God, but our life with God affects our life in the world. Christian living centers in a "baptism" of the common rather than in a separation from it. But because our life in the world affects our life with God, genuine confrontation with God is always mitigated by our own distorted mental images. Nevertheless, God is not only the God circumscribed in our mental images—he is, as Tillich says, the "God beyond God." He "breaks through" these distorted images, and insofar as he does, he imparts a sense of direction and a sense of values. As an event in the life of the believer, this "breakthrough" of God moves him to interpret all other events within the context of *this* event. He is inspired to evaluate all situations in terms of *this* situation. Since God's breakthrough in the life of the believer is the reflection of his breakthrough in the incarnation, its influence can be interpreted in the light of this central breakthrough.

As the redemptive work of Christ took place in time and yet encompassed the eternal, so God's breakthrough in the life of the believer is in time and yet encompasses the eternal. Life with God adds an eschatological dimension to life. Here we have a clue to the nature of the "difference." The difference lies in the eternal dimension within which the believer sees the issues of his life. The believer, by the very fact that he is a believer, allows for the eschatological dimension in what is transpiring at the moment. This dimension is essentially the faith that God's eternal purposes are being revealed in the present moment of existence. Sustained by his relationship with God, the believer's qualitatively different way of seeing extends his ordinary life to a significance not possible without it. "Blessed are the eyes which see what you see!" (Luke 10:23). We see them, not because of anything substantially different in the object of our sight, but because of a substantial difference in the nature of our seeing. Our belief in Christ creates an existential difference in the quality of our perception. It is the awareness of a committed person that the one to whom he is committed is at hand. Instead of "leaning on our own understanding," we "acknowledge him in all our ways."

The present tense can incorporate the eternal dimension only because the future holds the key to the ultimate meaning of what has already come upon us. The collect for the Third Sunday after Trinity asks for God's help that "we may so pass through things temporal that we lose not the things eternal." The petition has both a present and a future reference, since we can lose the things eternal now in the present temporal moment as well as in the life to come. Yet both meanings of the eternal are essentially one, if either is more than a mere abstraction. If the future hope is really a hope, it affects the way one views the present, and if one views the present with an eternal as well as a temporal dimension, it is only because he has hope that there is in the present that which "does not pass away."

This eschatological dimension of life is described by Tillich as "the creation into eternity out of every moment of time."[6] Each moment is therefore the potential *kairos* —a moment pregnant with unlimited possibilities—in contrast to a purely *chronos* interpretation of time—time as a chronological process. This is essentially the distinction between the Hebrew and Greek concepts of time. For the Hebrews each day was unique, having no impersonal forces determining its limits, not even a law of averages. In contrast, the Greek concept subjected each moment of time to a mechanistic and cyclic type of futility. In the Christian outgrowth of the Hebrew tradition, God speaks to the believer and the believer responds to God in the "eternal now." This is the indescribable and qualitative difference between the common, natural life and the Christian life—a difference which consists in the baptism of the existential moment in the life experience, a moment in which the believer both receives and gives, a situation in time that is opened to eternity.

The Christian, therefore, is the same as any other person, except, as Luther says, he is *in grace.* But being *in grace,* as we have seen, he is not the same. Yet the difference cannot be distinguished by the senses. There is nothing about it that would enable one to recognize, distinguish, or judge it without danger of error. But there is a difference—an extraordinary difference, as the Epistle to Diognetus says. As a "different" person, the Christian creates a different environment. He interacts with others in a way that produces a different effect. Paul attempts to describe this difference by naming the fruit of the Spirit—a list of virtues found in part in the philosophies of the Stoics and Epicureans, which Paul here places within a Christian setting and attributes to the Holy Spirit. Also in what appears to be an ethical reflection upon the redemptive love of Christ he composed his hymn of love which describes the disposition of the *different.* There is no doubt—Galatians 5:22 and 1 Corinthians 13 spell out specific and definite qualities of living.

> But the fruit of the Spirit is love, joy, peace, patience, kindness, goodness, faithfulness, gentleness, self-control; against such there is no law (Gal. 5:22-23).
> Love is patient and kind; love is not jealous or boastful; it is not arrogant or rude. Love does not insist on its own way; it is not irritable or resentful; it does not rejoice at wrong, but rejoices in the right. Love bears all things, believes all things, hopes all things, endures all things (1 Cor. 13:4-7).

There is nothing vague or even poetic about this description of love. Yet it is one thing to say that 1 Corinthians 13 describes the meaning of love and another to say that this or that person's example is a description of love. It may also be a description of something else.

Love will move toward these attributes of 1 Corinthians 13. Yet how well we succeed depends in part on where we begin. Some have more natural predisposition through constitution or environment toward these attributes than others. Also, some who are neither arrogant nor rude may be motivated more by the need to please than by love. Others may not insist on their own way because they are timid rather than loving. Still others may not be irritable or resentful, because they have repressed their hostility and their attributes are overcompensations for this fact. Love is patient and kind, but not all that looks like patience or kindness is love.

There is an element of the elusive about the divine influence in life. The effects of this influence are manifested because the influence is present, but the influence is not present because the effects are manifested. These effects can also be simulated. One cannot usher in the divine influence by imitating its manifestations, any more than he can identify it by its manifestations. In Jesus' parable of the separation of the sheep from the goats it is not only the goats that are bewildered by the nature of their indictment, but the sheep are just as amazed by the nature of their vindication. Even as the goats were unable to recall when they had not fed the hungry Christ or given him to drink, the sheep were unable to recall when they had done so. Their bewilderment is accounted for primarily by Jesus' explanation that inasmuch as they had done these things unto the least of his brethren, they had done them unto him. But it is a mistake to assume that this explanation accounts for all of their bewilderment. His ways are simply not our ways.

Rarely are we conscious of the divine influence we are exerting. In seeking to simulate the manifestations of this influence—like feeding the hungry—we anticipate commendation from Christ and gratitude from people. But when the right hand does not know what the left hand does (not when it knows and is trying to forget, but when it does not know), the divine life may be exerting its influence. Here also is an explanation for the bewilderment of the sheep. The discrepancy between exerting a Christian influence and being aware of this exertion may account for our frequent irritations toward the recipients of our "charity" for their lack of appreciation and gratitude.

To let God be God means to allow mystery beyond the perceptive. His signs are signs for faith and not for sight. He works "faith when and where he pleases,"[7] independent of signs, for it is signs and sight that go together, not signs and faith. By faith we may believe that God is using our life for the sanctification of life in this world, even as we may believe (by faith) that by his grace he is sanctifying us. How else can one entertain angels *unawares?* Our problem is that we want to identify the angels, preferably beforehand, but at least in retrospect. Ours is a *lust* to *know.* We desire to separate the supernatural from the natural for purposes of identification. If one has his choice, would he not prefer to walk by sight rather than by faith?

Behind this desire is our cultural fetish for getting results. Everything must prove itself or be set aside. Ours is a production-centered culture. What once characterized the business world now also characterizes the church. We know how to test for results in stewardship, in evangelism, in Christian education. Why not also for sanctification? But God will not sacrifice the supernatural to our desire to tabulate it. Actually this is a lust to possess it, to control it. In effect this desire is really the desire to possess and control God—"to be as God." It is an attempt to escape the dependence of the creaturely status. Barth states the case clearly. "To be sure, we can indeed make offering with our action, and we are invited to do this, but that by this we are Abel and not Cain is a thing not within our own power."[8] It is not within our own power because we are accepted by grace, and grace is not of our own doing.

In the natural there is the supernatural. But it is not an object for sight; rather it is a stimulus to faith. Faith is a dynamic within the sphere of the Spirit's encounter with man. It is within this elusive and yet definite supernatural penetration that the believer lives his natural existence. The Spirit sanctifies us in his own way and in his own time. Our faith that he sanctifies us cannot be dependent on our perception of his results. In fact, faith by its very nature is not dependent upon results—and the Spirit works through faith. Despite its deceptive appearance of passivity, faith is active in a very positive way. Trust in God is motivation for action. Bultmann puts it poetically—"In every moment slumbers the possibility of being the eschatological moment. You must awaken it."[9]

Footnotes

1. "The Epistle to Diognetus," Ancient Christian Writers, Vol. VI (London: Longmans, Green & Co., 1948), p. 138.
2. Ibid., p. 139.
3. June Bingham, "Reinhold Niebuhr in Detroit," Christian Century, March 8, 1961, p. 296.
4. Charles Merrill Smith, How to Become a Bishop Without Being Religious (New York: Doubleday & Co., 1965), p. 31.
5. Calvin, Institutes (Philadelphia: Presbyterian Board of Publication and Sabbath School Work), Vol. II, p. 221.
6. Paul Tillich, The New Being (New York: Scribner's, 1955), p. 24.
7. Augsburg Confession. The Book of Concord (Philadelphia: Fortress Press, 1959), p. 31.
8. Barth, The Holy Ghost and the Christian Life (London: Frederick Muller, Ltd., 1938), p. 69
9. R. Bultmann, The Presence of Eternity (New York: Harper & Row, 1957), p. 155.

CHAPTER SIX

Human Effort and Sanctification

The dynamics of involvement extend beyond the setting for this involvement to include the person—his initiative, courage, and self-affirmation. Involvement is a matter of giving as well as receiving. This poses a problem for sanctification. How is it possible to have human initiative in a Gospel of grace?

As human beings we desire to know the cause of things so we can control the effect. In the workings of divine grace upon us there is a cause, but this cause is not something which we can control. Can there be any place for human effort in our life with God when both cause and effect in this life are matters of grace?

Judging from the general tenor of the New Testament, the answer to our question would seem to be *yes.* Jesus said, "Be perfect." And again, "Seek ye first the kingdom of God." In the Letter to the Hebrews we are told to "strive for holiness." 1 John says, "All who keep his commandments abide in him." While Paul says that "God is at work in you, both to will and to work for his good

I. Grace or Effort

111

pleasure," he also says, "work out your own salvation with fear and trembling." He also says, "Let not sin therefore reign in your mortal bodies." The author of 2 Peter says, "Make every effort to make your calling and election sure." *Be, seek, strive, keep, let not, make every effort, work out*—all of these are imperatives. They challenge the will. They appeal to effort.

The simplest way to harmonize human effort and divine grace is to say that justification is an act of God alone while sanctification involves the believer's cooperation. While this answer has the advantage of simplicity, it separates justification and sanctification in a way that is theologically and experientially untenable. In effect, it denies the simultaneity of justification and regeneration. This "solution" rests upon a so-called "third use of the law." The first use is directed to the preservation of human society. The second use is to humble a man in preparation for his reception of the Gospel. The third use is a rule of life which the believer follows as a result of the power he has as a Christian. But does not a resort to law for sanctification deny the spontaneity of obedience which the Gospel supposedly evokes from the believer? Some would say yes and accuse the proponents of a third use of the law of being legalistic. Opponents of the third use in turn have been labeled "antinomian"—that is, those who would do away with all law in the Christian proclamation.

The question of responsibility is being raised also in the field of psychotherapy. Despite the fact that Freud had no intention of eliminating responsibility, there is a growing discontent with psychoanalysis for doing just this. Viktor Frankl's "Logotherapy," William Glassner's "Reality Therapy," and O. Hobart Mowrer's "Action Therapy" all fault psychoanalysis for putting so much emphasis upon the patient's past that his responsibility for the present remains unchallenged. The Statue of Liberty on our east coast, says Frankl, should be balanced by a Statue of Responsibility on our west coast. The critics further charge that in stressing unconscious conflicts, psychoanalysis has fostered a philosophy of unconscious determinism. It is not a man's *conditions* that are determinative, Frankl says, but his *decisions*. Because psychoanalysis seeks to undo repression, it removes the moral judgment upon behavior. The critics feel that this has tended to remove the patient from moral responsibility. The new movements stress the patient's responsibility for taking the necessary steps to meet his moral and spiritual obligations.

Psychoanalysis probably deserves this criticism. In emphasizing factors beyond the patient's responsibility, it has tended to make him a victim of these factors and his recovery a matter of the right therapy rather than his responsible behavior. Yet reform movements can become equally erroneous in the opposite direction. The action therapy of O. Hobart Mowrer is a case in point. Mowrer has identified himself with the religious world and feels that the church has sold its birthright to Freud. As a professor of psychology, he castigates both psychiatrists and clergy for talking about sickness rather than sin. Unless we face the demons, he says, we will not hear the angels. However, how does Mowrer propose that we face the demons?

Guilt, he says, is real. It is created by the conscience, which apparently is absolute. How, then, can we appease this conscience? Two misleading—even pernicious—answers are the Protestant "justification by faith" and the psychiatric "justification by insight." Mowrer proposes the theological equivalent of "justification by works." The works are confession—not just to God but to people—and "compensating good deeds."

Mowrer's God is the projection of the conscience into the universe. "Just as conscience eventually condemns and turns against ('attacks') us for pursuing an evil life style, so will conscience eventually approve and reward us for a better type of conduct."[1] Any personal relationship with this God is viewed with the suspicion of mysticism. "One can rebuild his life, in a constructive and satisfying way, along lines laid down by Christ's *ethical* teachings: but the notion of the "mystical" union with Christ, has, I submit, little value save as a topic for endless theological disquisition."[2] Mowrer prefers to refer to sins rather than sin, and focuses on correcting each sin with the appropriate good work.

The New Testament poses a problem for Mowrer's theology, and he concentrates his attack on Paul. Here, he says, we find the source for the errors of Luther and Calvin. He prefers James, who says that faith without works is dead. It takes James "only three and one-half pages to refute the essence of what Paul takes eighty-eight pages, or nearly a third of the New Testament, to say."[3] His problem, however, is really with Christ, for there is no place in Mowrer's position for a Christ who does something for us that we cannot do for ourselves. Man has the law within himself, and when he feels guilty over not keeping this law, he has the potential to satisfy this guilt. In opposing "cheap grace," Mowrer has fallen off the other side of the horse and opposes *grace*. That man could possibly be both determined and responsible, he dismisses as nonsense.[4]

The abhorrence of one extreme may push one into another. We have another illustration of this effect in the conflict between Wesley and his Methodists and Zinzendorf and his Moravians. Wesley was appalled at Luther's approach to the law in his commentary on Galatians, accusing him of "blasphemously speaking of good works and the law of God—constantly coupling the law with sin, death, hell or the devil; and teaching that Christianity delivers us from the law of God."[5] (Luther's remarks, however, were actually directed to the *second* use of the law whose purpose is to accuse.) Although Wesley had been nurtured by the Moravians in his spiritual rebirth, he later broke with them—accusing them of following Luther in their attitude toward the law. For Wesley no law meant no works. It is only a small step from this emphasis on law in the Christian life to a concentration on external manifestations of obedience. On the other hand, the Moravians' appreciation for the redemptive work of Christ could go to a sentimental if not romantic extreme. So long as one appreciated the atonement, concern over conduct at times became secondary.

The controversy between Wesley and Zinzendorf raises the question concerning how much we can emphasize a voluntary spontaneity in response to the Gospel. Will a person automatically show love to others because he has experienced love from God? (1 John 4:19). Or is this too idealistic for human nature? In addition to our response to the Gospel, there is also our defiance of this Gospel. If it *is* too idealistic, how much may we stress conformity through effort without returning again to an emphasis upon law? How much can we appeal to willpower in obeying religious and ethical directives in the face of inner resistance? Will we not then simply arouse this inner resistance and pit the self against itself?

The confusion of sanctification with justification was a source of theological conflict in the Reformation. Through the infused grace of the sacramental system, the faithful in Catholicism were supposedly given power to do good works that were meritorious for salvation. The Reformers broke with this system because they believed

**II.
Abuse
of
Safeguards**

it denied the sufficiency of Christ's atonement. It is the atonement that justifies, they maintained, and only out of this justification which one already possesses can good works proceed. But even in the churches of the Reformation it has proved difficult to inspire people to good living without making sanctification a hidden qualification for justification.

Luther relied on the formula, "justification by faith alone." But in contrast to Luther, how often has faith been distorted in Lutheran circles to mean something that one conjures up within himself to qualify for salvation. Instead of worrying over whether he has done enough good works to be saved, the believer worries over whether he has enough faith. So faith becomes the good work and human effort the means for obtaining it. A new wording is obviously needed—justification by faith *in God alone* and not by faith *in faith alone.* But no correct formulation can guarantee the preservation of the truth it represents. In fact, its adherents may seek to qualify for justification by possessing this correct formulation, which then would become the equivalent for faith.

In his doctrine of predestination Calvin went one step farther than justification by faith to safeguard the monergism of divine grace. If one's salvation or damnation has been determined from all eternity, it certainly is not contingent upon his works done in his life. In fact, the very fatalism implied in predestination may lead to the opposite effect, namely, to a carelessness about maintaining good works. To counteract this, Calvin strongly stressed the third use of the law, which he insisted was its primary use. In following God's law, the Christian was not only giving evidence to others that he was one of God's elect but also giving assurance to himself. In other words, the best way to know you are one of the elect is to act like one. This need for reassurance concerning how one had been predestined led also to a strong emphasis upon signs of divine favor. Although he worked hard in his occupation to glorify God, the success he achieved through his efforts reassured the believer that God was with him. So Max Webber and others have associated the establishment and success of modern capitalism with the Calvinist emphasis on work—a covert expression of *work* righteousness.

Later the Wesleyan movement added another emphasis in Protestantism—an emphasis on feelings and love. Wesley reinforced justification by faith by describing faith as a heart-warming experience and by identifying it in the activity of love. As Harald Lindstrom has pointed out in his study *Wesley and Sanctification,* though Wesley placed the source of sanctification in the motive rather than in the act of love, this double emphasis upon the experiential witness of the Spirit and the tangible fruit of the Spirit led him to believe that if one judged himself by these marks of sanctification he ran little risk of deceiving himself regarding his motivations.[6] Once self-deception is minimized it is an easy step to Wesley's doctrine of perfection.

When we desire to produce tangible results—and the desire is rather universal—it is amazing how theological presuppositions that might interfere with this desire are ignored. The old conflict between Pelagius and Augustine has been settled in favor of Augustine so far as official ecclesiastical positions are concerned. But Pelagius' teaching about the potential in human effort is hard to resist when we want to inspire people to action. Says G. W. H. Lampe, "The pulpit orator, if he finds it necessary to exhort his congregation to practical morality, is always inclined to sound Pelagian even if he be St. Augustine in person."[7] Granted that such appeals may be based upon the hearer's need to maintain or establish the justification

that he has by grace, do they not still make this justification ultimately dependent upon human effort? Even if
we avoid the legal basis by appealing to the need to please
the God who has given so much to save us, are not such
appeals a sign of the failure of God's saving love to evoke
a response, so that it must be implemented by appeals to
please? Where is the genuineness of spontaneity in all of
this? And are we not really appealing to guilt rather than
to love?

In his attack on the scholastic Latomus, Luther tried to
solve this problem by making a distinction between grace
and faith on the basis of Romans 5:15, "But the free gift
is not like the trespass. For if many died through one man's
trespass, much more have the grace of God and the free
gift in the grace of that one man Jesus Christ abounded
for many." Because the "grace of God" and the "free
gift" are separated by the Apostle, Luther identified grace
as the outward good of God's favor in contrast to his
wrath (justification), and the free gift as the inward good
of faith, which purges the sin to which it is opposed (sanctification). Grace as the first foundation is stronger and
more important than faith. Although faith amounts to
something, it does so only through the power of grace.[8]
Contrasting faith as an inward gift with grace as an outward state of favor preserves the unity of faith with grace,
but the problem remains in what way human effort is
related to the results of the gift—the inward purging of
sin.

III.
Covenant
Mutuality

A more decisive role for human effort is contained in
the covenant concept of sanctification in which the mutuality of both parties to the covenant is stressed. In both
the old and new covenants, God initiates the covenant
and the people of God commit themselves in loyalty to it.
Such a commitment influences behavior. The covenant

relationship implies obligation. The "elect" have been given all—and therefore are expected to give all. As committed persons, we have burned our bridges behind us, and our life is not our own. The plural "our" is not incidental. While the concept of justification by faith has an individualistic reference, the concept of the covenant relationship includes a social emphasis. Arising out of the old covenant's emphasis upon Israel as the people of God, the new covenant is related to the new Israel—the holy catholic church. The covenant concept does not simply refer to the believer in the covenant relationship with God but to the believer as a member of a body of believers who are committed together. The group supports and inspires the loyalty of the individual. In spite of this advantage, the Old and New Testaments continually contrast God's fulfillment of his end of the covenant with the unfaithfulness of the people of God in their responsibilities.

As mediators of the new covenant between God and his people, the Sacraments of the church illustrate this two-way commitment. Baptism is a sign and a means for God's bestowal of grace. As the recipient of this grace, the one who is being baptized commits himself to God (in the presence of the body of believers). In the case of an infant, his parents or sponsors declare the child's covenant obligations for him. In the Lord's Supper, the bread and wine are signs and means of God's giving of himself. The recipients in turn offer themselves to God. The commitment is given both in the participant's declaration of intention to amend his sinful ways in the preparatory confessional, and in his very act of joining with his fellow participants in the celebration of the Sacrament. Stimulated by God's own act of sacrifice, the participants "present [their] bodies as a living sacrifice" (Rom. 12:1).

This responsibility of the believer toward God justifies the seriousness with which he takes his own efforts. The importance of our work is reflected by our covenant responsibilities. Its importance in our prayers and in our general concern may be more than mere egocentricity. One may have a sense of his own importance because of his need for status and the egocentric illusion over his own indispensability. However, he may also have this sense of importance because he is committed to One greater than himself and must "prove his own work" as his covenant responsibility. There is a tight-rope tension between taking one's responsibility seriously because he is covenanted to God and doing so because in his megalomania he has overrated his own importance under the *illusion* of responsibility to God. Despite this tension, the difference still exists.

IV.
Loyalty
and the
Will

In the covenant idea the faith which justifies and the love which results are expressions of loyalty to God. This is especially apparent when faith and love have internal opposition. In the face of such opposition, Paul directs us to "punish every disobedience" (2 Cor. 10:6). This is comparable to Luther's concept of purging out our sin—the work of the *gift* of God, namely, our faith. *Punishing all disobedience* is born out of a hatred for sin as God's enemy. Behind it is the "readiness" or determination to be loyal. Only as we confront our own inner opposition will our determination be sufficient to punish all disobedience.

We see this in Jesus' story of the man who had two sons. He asked the one to work in the vineyard and he refused. Later he repented and went. He asked the other son likewise to go to work and he said he would. But he never went. The son who said no but later went faced his opposition openly. He allowed himself the freedom to rebel. But having claimed this freedom, he realized it was not what he really wanted. With the alternative so honestly before him, he chose to be loyal to his father. He took his filial relationship too seriously to allow himself to gloss over his real feelings about it.

The other son lived in a pipedream. Refusing to face his resistance to his father, he chose to think that he was loyal. So he easily agreed with what his father asked him to do. But somehow he never got around to doing it. How could he so readily dismiss the matter? Kierkegaard says that the very same second that a person knows what to do and does not do it, "the knowledge stops boiling."[9] Behind the delay is the question of how the *will* rather than the intellect reacts to this knowledge. If it reacts negatively, it does not usually rebel openly. Rather it permits the passage of time to obscure the knowledge. In other words, the will distracts our attention from the knowledge until the knowledge fades away. In the case of the second son, he simply did not take his obligation to his father seriously enough to warrant *any* decided action. He lived in the pipedream that discerning the good was of some value in itself so that acting upon it could safely occupy his secondary attention.

Bonhoeffer's insight into the inner dynamics of Phariseeism is enlightening at this point. The Pharisee's knowledge is the knowledge of good and evil that he "gained" from the fall. As such it is indicative of the disunity within himself. Because he possesses this knowledge, he is preoccupied with making value judgments concerning himself and others. These judgments rarely lead to any further action. In contrast, when one is in covenant relationship with God through Christ, his knowledge is readily transferred into action because it is primarily a knowledge of knowing. His will is unified in commitment to this one whom he knows. He is so far removed from preoccupation with value judgments that his own goodness is concealed from him as he concentrates upon the one important thing—the will of God.[10]

God works through the decision and subsequent effort of those who are covenanted to him. Commitment leads to immediate action. It is the power behind such exorcisms as "Get thee behind me, Satan," and "Resist the devil and he will flee from you," and "One little word o'erthrows him [Satan]." The opposite of "one little word" is struggle. In simple decision there is clarity; in struggle there is the cloudiness of self-deception. The very fact that one engages in a struggle is indicative of his resistance to making any "either-or" decision. Instead of rebelling decisively, he rebels indecisively. By appearing more helpless in the face of temptation, he can more easily live with his duplicity. Struggling strengthens the adversary. Rather than being an alternative to succumbing to temptation, it is an alternative to rejecting temptation. By struggling, he keeps the issue alive without openly willing to do so —and this is precisely what he desires.

Cravings and addictions, from kleptomania to biting one's nails, reveal this surreptitious ambivalence. Victory over the addiction has its beginning when the individual realizes his fight is against himself—a fight he is doomed to lose because a house divided against itself shall fall. As one counselee expressed it, "Although I no longer live with my parents, I've got them inside of me—saying no. And just like when I was home—this simply makes me want to do it."

This insight reminds us of what Paul said about the negative effect of the law. "Our sinful passions, aroused by the law . . . finding opportunity in the commandment, deceived me" (Romans 7:5, 11). The law within us is identified with the authorities against whom we are rebelling. Though the law is also within us, it still has the aura of external control. Our revolt, then, is a negative expression of our freedom and its preservation. The aforesaid counselee was somewhat aware of this.

Counselee: I think I get satisfaction out of getting away with it.

Pastor: One side of you plays tricks on the other.

Counselee: I remember once telling myself, "Do you really want to? Go ahead, if you do." Then I seemed to lose interest.

Pastor: Once you gave yourself the freedom, you were not sure you really wanted it.

The dynamic described in this excerpt is what Frankl calls "paradoxical intention"—a major factor in his logotherapy. One's unapproved self functions with no communication with the approved self. Pressure upon the approved self always precipitates counter-pressure from the unapproved self. In our obsessive, compulsive, and phobic conditions, we tend to overrate the power of the adversary—to deify the devil. Instead, says Frankl, we should ridicule him—make light of the threats. Such tactics, however, will only work when the person is committed to a purpose for living that goes beyond himself. Instead of fighting the obsession, he may will to do it. When there is nothing to fight, the counselee may discover that his problem is over.

While there is new freedom in the cessation of inner struggle, paradoxical intention also has its limitations. The emotions can be very overwhelming and triggered into sabotage at the most unpredictable moments. Yet the principle has relevance for pastoral counseling. People expect the pastor as the authority to reinforce their acceptable self against their unacceptable self. His pressure then simply reinforces the counter-pressure. But what if he does not exert pressure? The counselee then has an unexpected freedom. When there is no authority to resist, the unacceptable self has no reason for existence. In his subsequent reorientation, the person may realize that he does not have as much desire for the "unapproved" as he had feared. As our counselee said, "When I came here I expected you as a pastor to bolster my willpower, and then when you didn't, it bothered me. It seemed that you were saying I could do what I wanted. I realized then that *I* had to decide—that I *could* decide—either way. It seemed to change the whole picture."

The divided will is an indication of egocentricity. When a person has no commitment beyond his own self, this self disintegrates. It cannot endure the responsibility of being its own god. In its disunity, the will may be divided into a good and an evil will, but the good is really a distortion of the good and the evil is a distortion of the evil, and the divided will leads to stalemate. "The doubleminded man [is] unstable in all his ways" (James 1:8). On the other hand, "purity of heart is to will one thing."[11] Idolatrous worship may unite the will temporarily to evil, but God alone can unite the will to the genuinely good by provoking the response of commitment to the covenant. Jeremiah describes the new covenant action as God's writing his law on the hearts of men. Paul describes it as "the mind of Christ in us." More than a converted will, it is a new will. Since the new man lives only in relationship to the God who has covenanted with him, we can say that in a very real way Christ is *in* us. He is formed in us (Gal. 4:19) as we by his Spirit are conformed to him. Yet the decisions that we make in our covenant commitment are *our* decisions, and the action that we take is *our* action.

V.
The
Need
to
Constrain

In one of the recorded post-resurrection appearances of Christ, two of his disillusioned followers were joined by a third party as they walked to Emmaus. Not recognizing him, they told him about the crucifixion of Jesus and of the disturbing rumors about his resurrection. When they drew near Emmaus, the stranger "appeared to be going further." However, they "constrained" him to lodge with them over night since it was toward evening. As the stranger broke the bread at the table, their eyes were opened and they recognized him.

A strange story from the Old Testament follows a similar pattern. As the patriarch Jacob was left alone in his fearful trek back to his homeland after twenty years as a fugitive, a man wrestled with him until the break of day. When the man asked him to let him go, Jacob would not except the man bless him. When Jacob asked him his name, the man asked why he wanted to know. After he had been blessed, Jacob called the place "the face of God," for, he said, "I have seen God face to face, and yet my life is preserved." Charles Wesley had caught the import of the experience in verse:

> Yield to me now, for I am weak,
>   But confident in self-despair;
> Speak to my heart, in blessing speak,
>   Be conquered by my instant prayer.
> Speak, or thou never hence shalt move,
> And tell me if thy name is Love.
>
> SBH, 471:4

Like Jacob the Emmaus disciples sensed that there was something about the stranger that suggested the divine. After their "eyes had been opened" they said to one another, "Did not our hearts burn within us while he talked to us on the road, while he opened to us the scriptures" (Luke 24:32). And in the blessing that Jacob and the Emmaus disciples received the nature of the mysterious figure was revealed.

> 'Tis Love, 'tis Love, thou died'st for me!
> I hear thy whisper in my heart!
> The morning breaks, the shadows flee;

Pure universal love thou art;
To me, to all, thy mercies move;
Thy nature and thy name is Love.

SBH, 471:5

Although the street crowd told him to be quiet, Bartimaeus, the blind beggar of Jericho, cried out all the more to attract the attention of Jesus who was passing by —and finally succeeding, he received his sight. The Syrophoenician woman was told by Jesus that he had come only to the lost sheep of the house of Israel and that it was not fair to take the children's bread and to cast it to dogs. Yet, she persisted in the face of such discouragement and received healing for her daughter, and the compliment, "O woman, great is your faith" (Matt. 15: 28).

God expects us to constrain him. But the effort we put forth is in the nature of a response. The stimulus is from God. Our response is evoked. Even if he appears to be going farther or asks to be released from the wrestling before daybreak, he is still beckoning to us. We are like plants growing toward the sun. In one sense the plant is reaching out to the sun; in another sense the sun is pulling the plant toward it. Yet if the light were not shining upon it, the plant could not grow toward it. Like all analogies, this too has its limitations. The response of the plant is inherent in its nature; the response of the human being can be resisted by the human being. There is no reason to believe, for example, that those would-be disciples whom Jesus challenged with stumbling-blocks ever persisted. Even though one of them said he would follow Jesus wherever he went, when he was warned that the Son of Man had nowhere to lay his head, his ardor apparently cooled. The same was true for the one who first wanted to say goodbye to his family and was told that no man who puts his hand to the plow and turns back is fit for the kingdom of God. In both of these remarks Jesus gave the impression of departing, but obviously he desired to be constrained.

Or consider his appeal to Judas who thought no one knew of his traitorous contact with the chief priests. But in the upper room Jesus brought it into the open. After letting Judas know he knew what he was up to, Jesus said, "What you are going to do, do quickly" (John 13: 27). There was no challenge now to try to get away with something. Nobody was even going to try to stop him. He was now free to ask himself whether he really wanted to go through with it. It was Jesus' most effective appeal —but it failed. Although it is God who does the sanctifying, he works through the function of the human will.

When we put our emphasis upon the role of human effort in sanctification, there is usually a corresponding emphasis on programs for sanctification. These programs have the inherent danger of removing the focus from the God who is sanctifying to the activity of the one who is being sanctified. Regardless of how God-centered our theological descriptions of the program may be, the emphasis on the activity itself is a functional displacement in varying degree of the unpossessiveness of the Holy Spirit, and to this extent is an inhibitor of any genuine sanctification. This danger is present in all devotional exercises, from Brother Lawrence's practice of the presence of God to Frank Laubach's practice of the consciousness of God. Despite the depth of spirituality in Brother Lawrence, his program of sanctification centers on the human ability of *practicing* the presence of God. This produces all of the fine qualities of disposition that mysticism encourages, but it need not produce sanctification. Even the desire to dispense with all patterns can itself become a pattern. The quietist attempt to "think God" as

VI. Effort and Programs

an alternate to thinking *about* God is actually to produce a mental image of no mental image.

The same criticism can be made of the asceticism at the basis of the religious community. The emphasis upon ascetic activity is as common among non-Christian religions as it is in the Christian religion, and is just as likely to produce a caricature of Christian perfection as the real thing. In becoming stereotyped, any program ceases to be of the Spirit but rather of the flesh, that is, it becomes a high form of human aspiration and attainment. Since physical exercises result in stronger muscles, spiritual exercises ought also to result in stronger spirits. Perhaps they do. But a strong spirit and a sanctified spirit are not necessarily the same.

The fact that no pattern of human activity can produce a sanctified person points to the sovereignty of the Spirit's sanctifying work. The element of predestination in the Christian kerygma is a warning against any pattern that guarantees sanctification. Even a formula that preserves the *monergism* of divine grace can be made *synergistic* by the way it is used. Every attempt to describe what we mean by sanctification and how we achieve it contains within itself the danger of reducing the mystery of the divine act. The door is opened for the human desire to possess God—to "tack him down"—to control him.

Although the English Puritans more than any others developed the covenant concept of sanctification, their ascetic tendencies led them to interpret the covenant committal in terms of a series of directives. In his *Directions and Persuasions to a Sound Conversion*, for example, Richard Baxter gives the directives for fulfilling our covenant responsibilities. They can be summed up as follows:

1. Labor for a right understanding of Christianity.
2. When you have this understanding, search the Scripture to see if it be so.

3. Be much absorbed in your religious thoughts.
4. Humiliate the spirit in contrition, but do not over-do this point.
5. Keep close to Christ.
6. Thoroughly mortify the flesh, showing contempt for the world.
7. Be sure to make resignation of yourself to God.
8. Do not mistake a mere change for a saving change.
9. Acquaint yourself with the Christian life, letting your heart be in the right place.
10. Do not do the above to avoid punishment.
11. Turn today!
12. Do not dabble here and there but make the Christian life the habitual state of your soul.

There is a similar series of directives in his *Discourse for Weak and Distempered Christians* and *Right Method for a Settled Peace of Conscience.*

While these steps can be identified with the sanctification process—and probably were in a man like Baxter, who could say, "I can as willingly be a martyr for love, as for an article of the creed"[12]—they need not be. They represent the danger of taking a specific insight or experience from one's own "walk with God" and generalizing upon it. Only God—not our idea of God, our effort to remain close to God, or even our trust in God—is the object of our trust. Otherwise the very insight that we have received will detract from God. Something less than God is elevated to God's place and no matter how wise and pious and spiritual this something is, it is of necessity an attribute of the flesh.

Even Luther's theology of the cross is no formula for growth. The crucifixion or death experience is actually a despair over all programs for improvement, formulas for sanctification, and exercises for spiritual growth. Only suicide remains as an escape from the dilemma. In dying to the old nature the person dies to himself and all the recourses he might have for changing things—leaving only a miracle, a resurrection, as the way out. The believer contributes neither to his crucifixion nor to his resurrection, for both are the work of the Spirit. Our attempts to stimulate either the crucifixion of the old or the resurrection of the new merely distort and falsify. He who desires a cross is not really desiring a cross. The very nature of a cross is denied by the fact that it is desired. On the other hand, if one could bring about his resurrection, he might well question whether he had died. For both the crucifixion and the resurrection we wait upon the Lord. But our trust is not in our waiting, but rather in the Lord.

The Christian hope is that God "who began a good work [in us] will bring it to completion" (Phil. 1:6). Patterns for sanctification depend on progress. Progress, of course, is necessary—but not the *awareness* of progress. Actually awareness of progress is the greatest threat to progress because humility is involved in sanctification and awareness of progress is an obstacle to humility. As one may lose his humility when he claims it, so he may endanger his progress in sanctification when he becomes aware of it. Progress in sanctification may be something to believe (faith) rather than to see (sight). The way of sanctification is revealed more in the crisis of defeat than in the gradualism of progress.

There is a difference between hungering and thirsting for righteousness and coveting it. The ideal of righteousness may be a form of ego image. The desire to be saintly may be the desire to think more highly of oneself—essentially a lust of the flesh. The Gospel then is an offense because it centers in forgiveness, and forgiveness is something such a person is interested in *not needing* rather than in *receiving*. The coveted image of goodness may be the flesh's way of resisting the cross—of avoiding its own crucifixion.

Those who covet the image of goodness are seeking a character trait rather than their sanctification. The character trait is often the opposite of a particular character weakness which they have learned to despise. So great is the disdain that sin itself is almost identified with the particular weakness. Life in the Roman Empire during the third century of the Christian era abounded in luxury, carousal, and sexual promiscuity. Saint Anthony began a movement to escape such a life. He retreated to solitude in the deserts of Egypt and became known as the first Christian monk. As a result, sin became identified with a life of carnal indulgence in the physical appetites, and its opposite, the ascetic life, the epitome of virtue. If one is bedeviled by sexual lust, mastering sex may be tantamount to overcoming sin in his life. Perhaps instead his primary identification with sin is in his temper. Then the coveted character trait would be an irenic disposition. If it is worry and fretting, then the ideal is to become carefree. If it is an inferiority complex that is despised, one's goal might then be to achieve a confident spirit. If one is an alcoholic, sobriety may be his symbol for all that is good.

When we identify sanctification with the achievement of specific character traits, our understanding of sin and righteousness becomes distorted. Even when the character trait is achieved, the person may be no nearer the kingdom of God than before. He *may* be nearer, but he may also be farther removed. The wisdom of the Alcoholics Anonymous movement is that its program goes beyond sobriety to spiritual development. Yet in contrast to the tangible nature of sobriety, no twelve steps can be counted upon to produce spiritual development.

When we think of sin in terms of a specific weakness

our great desire is to overcome this weakness. If by the use of some wise pattern of behavior one begins to conquer this weakness, his joy may become mixed with a vague sort of fear. If he could put it into words, it would go somewhat like this: "If I should conquer this besetting sin, what worlds would I have yet to conquer? Is it possible that I will have arrived! If so, I am not sure that I really like the idea." This apprehension can lead us to sabotage our own progress. The very perfection we supposedly desire, we also fear. In contrast to the constantly guilty feeling we have known, the victory would lead us into "virgin territory." Could we endure it? What would be the consequences for our humility? What further need would we have for repentance? The very fact that we could entertain such apprehensions shows how concentrating on a specific sin distorts our understanding of sin. It also shows how shallow is the image we have of ourselves.

VII.
Commitment
and
Sanctification

The power for sanctification comes through taking God seriously. Then we are no longer interested in power but in our covenant responsibilities. The egocentric person seeks power, even for good purposes. In contrast, the covenant commitment is stimulated by response love. Herein is its creative power as love expresses itself in action. One is conscious, not of power, nor even of faith, but of God and the covenant obligations to him. So the divine—God's covenant overture—enters the human through the interaction of love and sanctifies the human through this involvement.

The love response to the covenant of love is expressed through the medium of worship. All of our insights into sanctification are inseparable from this unique involvement of the creature with his Creator. Separated from this encounter, these same insights become sterile and distorted. This is why they cannot be generalized or passed on as formulas. Yet history shows that this is precisely what we attempt to do. No description can in itself substitute for that which it describes. The dynamic involved is the loyalty of love in a committed life.

The ancient Greeks taught that man's salvation was in his powers of reason. They assumed that if the reason were operating, the will would naturally follow. They also apparently assumed that the reason was sovereign over the emotions. In both of these assumptions they overrated the autonomy of the reason, underrated the autonomy of the will, and had much to learn regarding the *sub-rosa* activity of the emotions. But when the integrating influence is our covenant relationship to God, it affects all aspects of our person. The commitment that involves the will embraces a faith that influences the reason and a personal dimension that affects the emotions.

A pastoral theology that is based upon the involvement of commitment influences the nature of pastoral care. Since the pastor is a committed person, his pastoral counseling is more than problem-solving. While it may come into being as a result of the counselee's problem, the pastor's responsibility in his counseling goes beyond this immediate sense of need. The prophetic ministry can no more be separated from the pastoral counseling ministry than sanctification can be sacrificed to problem solving. The counselee has responsibility, not only for his own self-fulfillment or for the fulfillment of his marriage, but also for his neighbor in terms of the corporate structures of our society. Beyond his responsibility to the counselee's sense of need, the pastor is responsible for confronting the counselee with his responsibility to the social order in his vocation as a Christian—for the Christian lives not unto himself but unto the Christ to whom he is committed through death and resurrection. This is his sanctification.

Footnotes

1. O. Hobart Mowrer, *Crisis in Psychiatry and Religion* (Princeton, N.J.: D. Van Nostrand Company, Inc., copyright 1961), p. 232.
2. *Ibid.*, p. 182.
3. *Ibid.*, p. 187.
4. *Ibid.*, p. 147.
5. Harald Lindstrom, *Wesley and Sanctification* (Naperville, Ill.: Allenson, 1946), p. 76.
6. *Ibid.*, p. 148.
7. Quoted in Mascall, *Recovery of Unity* (London: Longmans, 1958), p. 63.
8. "Against Latomus," *Luther's Works* (Philadelphia: Muhlenberg Press, 1958), Vol. 32, pp. 238-239.
9. Kierkegaard, *Sickness unto Death*. Trans. by Walter Lowrie (New York: Doubleday & Co., 1954), p. 225.
10. Bonhoeffer, *Ethics* (New York: Macmillan Co., 1961), pp. 151-161.
11. Kierkegaard's theme in *Purity of Heart*.
12. *Baxter's Works* (New Haven: Jurrie & Peck, 1931), Vol. I, p. 264.

CHAPTER SEVEN

Knowing and Knowledge

Sanctification is not simply a matter of a person's behavior in society. As a religious process, sanctification pertains not just to life with people but to life with God. While the two are mutually related, they are not identical. Sanctification centers in *knowing* God, and this *knowing* is the basis for the morality in sanctification. Not all morality stems from religion and not all religion leads to morality. *Pure* religion, however, *does*—as James has said, "Religion that is pure and undefiled before God and the Father is this: to visit orphans and widows in their affliction, and to keep oneself unstained from the world" (1:27). Pure religion also consists in knowing the only true God. "This is eternal life, that they know thee the only true God, and Jesus Christ whom thou hast sent" (John 17:3).

Knowing a person from sense date alone is different from knowing him within a personal relationship. Tournier describes this difference as the difference between knowing the personage and the person. The personage can be

I. Knowing the Person

described, but only the person can be known. From the beauty and the order of nature, from the value structure of the conscience, even from one's mystical apprehension of the world of the spirit, the personage of God is known. But it is only as God chooses to reveal himself through these "masks" that we know his person. This he does in the intimacy of communion. He is one with whom we *walk*—a friend, father, confidant. There is much that is left to our imagination in filling in the gaps in our knowledge of God from his world of creation. The experience of *knowing* fills in these gaps.

Whitehead's familiar saying that "religion is what a man does with his solitude" is only a half-truth. To complete it we need Brunner's assertion that "he who believes is never solitary."[1] When God communicates his Person he communicates agape—the highest personal expression of knowing. Love provides its own understanding. We can hardly put into words what love has communicated to us. Yet we know. Next to John himself, Bernard of Clairvaux is the churchman most identified with the love of God—and as always this love is known rather than defined.

> But what to those who find? Ah, this
>   Nor tongue nor pen can show;
>   The love of Jesus, what it is,
>   None but his loved ones know.
>
> SBH, 481:4

But this does not mean that *knowledge* is unrelated to *knowing*. Knowing comes about through knowledge even as knowledge comes about through knowing. God's revelation of himself—his love—is accomplished in the context of the Gospel—which has historical roots and therefore can be communicated as knowledge. C. H. Dodd reduces the essentials of the Christian kerygma to the following events which can be learned as facts.

1. The prophecies of the Old Testament are fulfilled in the coming of Christ, born of the seed of David.
2. Christ died to deliver us from evil and was buried.
3. He rose on the third day.
4. He is exalted at the right hand of God from whence He will come again as Judge and Savior of men.[2]

Through this historical demonstration of agape which accomplished our redemption, we come to know him who is agape. God cannot be separated from his Gospel because it is through his Gospel that he is known. This association of God with the Gospel is the union of the Spirit with the Word. The Spirit without the Word removes God from the world of nature, time, and space, and the Word without the Spirit reduces the Gospel to historical knowledge and God to an idea. In this union of the Spirit with the Word, knowledge has a sacramental significance in that we receive the Spirit through the Word. It is through our knowledge about Christ that we learn to know Christ. We receive the love of God through the *story* of his love.

When we separate the Word from the Spirit the resultant holiness is that of the professional pundit. The most "holy" are the most learned. As the scribes of Jesus' day, they are like constitutional lawyers who go by the book—whether that book is the Bible or their own theological system. The popes of the Middle Ages, for example, were lawyers rather than theologians—medieval scribes of cannon law. Religion then is reduced to religious knowledge. But religious knowledge without the Spirit is simply one type of academic discipline among others. Religion may be just a frame of reference for the expression of a person's native predispositions and abilities. The successful president of the church women's society may just as readily be the successful president of the woman's civic club. The pastor who is an efficient administrator of his congregation may have been just as efficient as an executive in an insurance corporation, for he would be using the same talents. So the biblical exegete may have been just as authoritative and accurate as a student of ancient Egyptian manuscripts. The book can be mastered but not the Spirit. Being scholarly is not always the same as communicating the Word—for which more than intellectual concepts are required.

On the other hand, when we separate the Spirit from the Word we are left with the holiness of the professional mysticist. The most "holy" are those with most acutely developed powers of contemplation. Religion is reduced to religious experience. But religious experience without the Word easily degenerates into the natural contemplative capacity of human beings to monologue with themselves. Even as one may lose the Word through the objectification of religion as religious knowledge, so he may lose the Spirit through the subjectification of religion as religious experience. In either the subjective or the objective extreme we are no longer aware that "it is a fearful thing to fall into the hands of the living God" (Heb. 10:31).

The presence of God repels even as it attracts. So also does the Word of God and its incarnation in the person of Christ. The story of Christ's life is the story of this contrast in human response. The Pharisees armed themselves with the boast that they had Moses and the prophets and thought themselves well defended by the taunt, "Is the Christ to come from Galilee?" Hearing Jesus' invitation to separate himself from his material possessions to become his disciple, the rich young ruler turned and walked away, hoping that the geographical separation would deaden the sound of the Lord's words. Hard pressed by the rise of Jesus' religious influence over the people, some of his enemies sought to hide their feelings by resorting to flattery. "Teacher, we know that you are true, and care for no man; for you do not regard the position of men, but truly teach the way of God" (Mark 12:14). Mastering religious knowledge and mastering mystical techniques are other ways in which we establish our own rightness and maintain our control. But all of this is far removed from receiving the Holy Spirit and from knowing God—and therefore from sanctification.

Behind these defenses against knowing there is often a fear of intimacy. Intimacy means sharing, and sharing means exposure. There is something irrevocable about this sharing—something that binds one to the confidant. Some shy away from intimacy because they have been hurt by previous exposure. Others may feel they have too much to hide. Men particularly hide their feelings. The one exception is anger—the "masculine" emotion. But when it comes to weakness, fear, guilt, or even tenderness, men are chary about exposure. Obviously a certain reserve is needed to conceal these feelings. Perhaps this is one reason why more women than men seem to be religious. Women can be weak and frightened without societal censure. In fact, men may even welcome these feelings from women so that they can rise to the occasion as men. Being less defensive about their emotional weakness and having less to conceal, women are more open for sharing.

Since knowing God is an experience in intimacy, we refer again to its biblical analogy to marriage—the most intimate of human relationships. In both Old and New Testaments the word used to denote the most intimate expression of this marital intimacy—the sex relationship—is the same as the word for religious intimacy—*knowing*. The muscular activity and nerve sensations of sexual inter-

course serve as media for the symbolic experience of
marital intimacy. To *know* is to share until the two become one. Yet the partners remain individuals. In fact,
their individuality is strengthened by the experience. So
also the believer's individuality is strengthened rather
than weakened by his experience of oneness with God.

Obviously any reluctance to share—to expose oneself—
to be bound to another—is an obstacle to married life.
Sex then may become a substitute for knowing rather than
its intimate expression. So also the forms for religious intimacy may become substitutes for knowing. Some are
too honest for such pretense and chafe under it. Bishop
John A. T. Robinson may be one of them. In one respect
the Bishop's views as set forth in *Honest to God* may be
interpreted as an answer to his own and others' problems
over intimacy. As background for his religious honesty,
Robinson recalls his personal difficulty with the devotional
aspect of religion, specifically prayer. The traditional approach "rang no bell," but rather left him cold. He was
simply "not on it."[3] When he discovered a fellow student
at seminary who had the same difficulty, he was relieved
that he was not the only one out of step and felt less
guilty over being spiritually inadequate. Since that time
he has met others who felt the same way but hesitated
to question the traditional approach for fear of seeming
to be unspiritual. On behalf of these and kindred causes,
the Bishop has brought the problems into the open and
proposed answers compatible to modern society. The attempt to make Christianity compatible to modern man is
not simply the problem of intellectual concepts but may
include also the problem of justifying a religiousness not
characterized by intimacy. As so frequently happens, the
emotional needs of people antedate their intellectual
needs and even help to create them.

Even as the Christian kerygma leads to knowing God,

so knowing God makes the kerygma knowable. We understand the story of his love through receiving his love. It helps us to "make sense" out of what is at best non-rational—"turns on the light," "rings the bell," "makes the pieces fall into place." Concerning his religious experience Luther said, "This straightway made me feel as though reborn, and as though I had entered through open gates into paradise itself. From then on the whole face of Scripture appeared different."[4] Scripture appeared different because *he* was different. In his experience of God through the Gospel he had moved from the conviction of condemnation under God's wrath to the assurance of blessing under God's grace.

When there is a barrier preventing one from relating intimately with God, his perception of the Scripture may be influenced negatively. If the barrier is guilt, he sees in it primarily his own condemnation. If it is bitterness, he sees inconsistencies, contradictions, problems. If it is estrangement from others, he sees confusion and irrelevancy. As a colleague of mine said, "The Bible was full of impossible problems for me and the more I attacked these directly the more confused I became. Then through certain events in my life, my religion became more meaningful to me. These problems over the Bible still remain, although they seem to have slipped into perspective. I accept them, I guess."

Job had a similar experience. Out of the despair of his agony, he belabored the inconsistency and irrational arbitrariness of God's ways, and repeatedly asked for the opportunity to meet his divine adversary face to face that he might vindicate himself. When the Lord answered him "out of the whirlwind," he had his encounter—and the experience changed his whole attitude. His words show the effect of *knowing*. "I have uttered what I did not understand, things too wonderful for me, which I did not know. . . . I had heard of thee by the hearing of the ear, but now my eye sees thee; therefore I despise myself, and repent in dust and ashes" (Job 42:3-6). What before had been the occasion for doubt and despair (crucifixion) was now the occasion for faith and repentance (resurrection).

Because religious problems are fitting to the profession when consulting the clergy, a pastor is frequently approached by people who present a *religious* problem as an introduction to other problems. Yet, these *other* problems are also religious. When one is in despair over his marital problems, he may in all honesty say, "I can't make any sense out of religion." The cloud of confusion over his faith is symptomatic of the darkness that hangs over his marriage. His problem is a single problem on two fronts and any effective pastoral care must recognize this interconnection. When the pastor succeeds in helping him to re-establish his intimacy in either area, he is restoring communication also at the other.

The experience of *knowing* conditions the mind to assimilate the non-rational in life—even the potentially miraculous—in a scientifically oriented age, and to anticipate an eschatological hope even in a world-accepting age. Obstacles to belief have always been with us, but in themselves they are not decisive. All are exposed to them but only some are offended by them. The difference lies obviously within the individual or within his group. Belief is always a faith "in spite of" as well as "because of." *Knowing* in the religious area involves the whole person and not simply the intellect.

This totality in knowing can be illustrated even in knowing among people. Personality inventories such as the Minnesota Multiphasic Personality Inventory give certain indications of the person. Yet it is not possible to know the person from just his inventory profile. After several conversations with the person himself, one has the setting needed for interpreting the profile. Even in common parlance we say, "Now that I know him, I can believe it." The implication of this remark is that specific information about a person was incomprehensible before one actually knew him.

The same is true with self-knowledge. In pastoral counseling such self-knowledge is called insight. The pastor does not want this self-knowledge to be simply information that he gives to the counselee. To become insight, this knowledge must come also from the counselee's own experience. As Carroll Wise says, insight is "an emotional grasp of elements which comprise the personality."[5] Thus it is not simply knowledge or education, but a revelation into oneself that comes about through intimate involvement with oneself. The milieu that facilitates such insight is one's intimate involvement with another person—or with God.

Our reason operates on the basis of our experiences, so that the natural man is not able to understand the things of God because they are spiritually discerned. The natural man is being perfectly logical in rejecting the ideas and value judgments of those who are spiritually minded. By the same token, those who have come to know God are being perfectly logical in their acceptance of these ideas and value judgments. The difference between the two points of view centers in the qualitatively different basis in experience upon which the reason of each operates.

With the insight or knowledge that comes from knowing God the believer is able to assimilate the paradoxes of life. Even the problem of evil—the ever present argument against any positive attitude toward life—is taken into the faith by which the believer's rational processes operate. He can account for his assimilation of this problem and present this accounting to others. But the description itself can neither account for his assimilation nor duplicate it in another. Because the description of the assimilation cannot communicate the assimilation, it remains for others a theory based on assumptions—assumptions which may even defy the intellectual credulity of some. In the Second Letter to Timothy, Timothy is urged to continue faithfully in what he has learned and believed, "knowing from whom you learned it" (2 Tim. 3:14-15). It is impossible to separate what we believe from the relationships out of which this belief has come. Therefore when we describe our beliefs our description is by necessity inadequate. The relationships with God and man which sustain these beliefs cannot be communicated by words, and therefore the logic so clear to us may be anything but clear to a person who has no one "from whom he learned it."

Clement of Alexandria wrote much about the insight (*gnosis*) that goes beyond wisdom (*sophia*). Insight for Clement was that particular knowledge which is the possession of those who have been initiated into it through intimacy with God. All insight is also wisdom, but not all wisdom can be called insight—which stems more from a sense of wonder toward the divine than from the sharpness of the intellect or the development of disciplined reason. This sense of wonder involves the feelings as well as the intellect. Clement was attempting to establish a *Christian* gnosticism, and what he taught is but a commentary on the proverb, "The fear of the Lord is the beginning of wisdom, and the knowledge of the Holy One is insight" (Prov. 9:10). This knowledge is rational, existential, and empirical, and its possession means that the total person knows.

Stemming from the wonder of knowing God, Clement's understanding of insight is the key to the difference be-

tween wisdom literature as such and the wisdom literature
of the Bible. So far as human evaluation is concerned,
all such literature has its brilliant and its mediocre sections. There may even be similar thoughts and wordings.
The context, however, is different. The writers of the
biblical wisdom literature wrote in the awareness that
their insights were inextricably united with the worship
of God. For Paul this context surpasses all knowledge, because to know Christ is to know the love of Christ. As one
is rooted and grounded in this love, he has power to comprehend with all saints what is the breadth and length
and height and depth—to comprehend the magnitude of
the knowledge that opens to faith. Although this love is
ultimately beyond understanding, it is not beyond experiencing.

For the most part no religion could be built on the
teachings of Jesus. They are not that unique. According
to R. C. Zaehner, Oxford professor in comparative religion,
there is nothing in the Sermon on the Mount that could
not be paralleled in the Buddhist scripture. The Buddha
no less than Christ taught an ethics of self-denial and a
universal love extending even to the enemy. Wisdom,
even religious wisdom, is a sort of common possession.
But what is unique about Jesus is Jesus himself. In his
bloody sacrifice in the crucifixion and in his resurrection
in his body, says Zaehner, Christ fulfills not only the law
and prophets of Israel but also the prophecy of Zoroaster
of Persia and the sages of India.[6] The uniqueness of
Christianity is in the insight that comes through knowing
Christ in his redemptive activity—his agape. This qualitative difference can be known even though it cannot
be adequately mapped by the knower. Word symbols can
communicate only when they stimulate in the mind of the
receiver a mental image comparable to that in the mind
of the communicator.

Because of our scientific orientation our age is not particularly conducive to religious faith. There is an awareness of the need for faith, but we find it difficult to possess it. The religious interest, church attendance, and church expansion in America may be as much an indication of the desire for faith as the possession of it. Our age has an abundance of *knowledge* but a poverty of *knowing*. We have an example in the field of personal relations. There has never been so much recorded knowledge about people in psychology, sociology, and anthropology as there is today, and yet there are probably more isolated people in the crowds of humanity than ever. The same may be true in the religious life. It is easier in the atmosphere of our times to learn about—objectively—than it is to know in any personal and intimate way. The emotional isolation that affects our culture affects also our religious life.

Like any relationship, knowing God needs exercise for its preservation. Good friends who separate from each other may discover they are strangers when they meet again. When knowing fades, the knowledge it sustains becomes empty of significance, and we are vulnerable to all sorts of distortion and confusion. The caution to watch and pray has a specific relevance for this distortion in perception. *Watching* means being alert to our predisposition for short-sightedness and wrong-headedness. *Praying* is the exercise of our relationship with God through which our knowledge of God retains its dynamic character.

The need to exercise our relationship with God emphasizes the place for daily devotions in the dynamics of sanctification. For some, the daily practice of devotions is a holdover from a previous and more religiously naive age. There is something to be said for this point of view. The practice certainly does not fit into the schedule of our activist culture. Nor do our denominational devotional guides always deal with the pertinent issues of modern life. Yet in spite of these handicaps, the practice can contribute to the vitality of the religious life. We need times when we concentrate on our fellowship with God to the exclusion of other preoccupations. The practice does not confine our relationship with God to these times. On the contrary, the practice is more likely to make our relationship meaningful at other times.

Since we cannot separate the commandment to love God with all our heart from the commandment to love our neighbor as ourself, we cannot separate the dialogue with God from the dialogue with man. Genuine community among people requires people who are genuine in their own selfhood. As Kierkegaard said, "Nobody can become my self for me." The route is through crucifixion and resurrection, through despair and self-affirmation. The experience is an activity within the dynamic of faith and is the way an individual grows into selfhood. One grows into his own selfhood through knowing God. More than most Christian thinkers, Calvin understood the relationship between knowing oneself and knowing God. "No man can arrive at the true knowledge of himself, without having first contemplated the divine character, and then descended to the consideration of his own." But this interrelationship is a two-way affair. Knowing ourselves leads to an increasing knowledge of God, or, as Calvin put it, is "a considerable assistance toward finding him."[7]

III. Knowing and Empathy

Only one who is becoming a self can share with another to any degree of depth. Much of what is understood as fellowship is superficial in nature due to conflicts in relating to ourselves. Confronted by the redemptive love of the personal Christ, these hindrances to our own self-

acceptance are under attack. As they give way before
the force of forgiveness, our very selfhood becomes enlarged. It is this deepening of our own person that enables
us to relate on a deeper level to our neighbor. The same
forgiveness that enlarges our own self-awareness makes
it possible to know our fellowman. "A Christian man,"
says Luther, "lives in Christ through faith, and in his
neighbor through love. By faith he is caught up beyond
himself into God, and by love he sinks down beneath himself into his neighbor."[8]

Our identification with others grows out of Christ's
identification with us. He was in all points tempted as we
are so that he might be a merciful and faithful high priest,
who having been tempted, "is able to help those who are
tempted" (Heb. 2:18). His sorrow at the tomb of Lazarus
can be interpreted as a sharing in the sorrow of others.

At times love may have to appear to be without feeling
in order to carry out its intentions. Too often we confuse
love with indulgence. Love is not simply feelings. Our
fear of hurting or our reluctance to disappoint may be
more self-defensive than self-giving. Wisdom sees beyond
the present moment of pain to future values. Therefore
love is an expression of the wisdom of the intellect as
well as of the feelings of the heart. Even those who are
the objects of love may not recognize this love and even
resist it because of the momentary pain and disappointment it seems to be causing.

Yet love is not without feeling, and if it should degenerate into such, it would become the cold and passionless
approach of the Stoics. For this reason compassion is included in love as its clothing without which it loses its
humanness. In its human setting, agape, the divine love,
is expressed not apart from but along with eros, the
human love, and by this utilization, transforms eros. What

results is not a synthesis which destroys agape but agape within the context of tangible sensitivity.

We are indebted to Anders Nygren for showing the difference between agape and eros and the way in which eros can corrupt agape. Yet by defining agape in opposition to eros, Nygren's agape ceases to be incarnate. To defend his isolation of agape, he is forced to say that man in his fallen state has no value at all. Even when he is redeemed his attitude toward God cannot be that of agape but rather of faith, because agape is given only when its object does not warrant it. Obviously God *has* a value to us, and therefore Richard Niebuhr speaks of our love for him as eros, since it is a response love. But Nygren has eros on the natural level and agape on the divine level and the two cannot meet without the corruption of agape.

Since the Johannine writings in the New Testament pose a problem to his system in their emphasis on the believer's agape for God, Nygren believes that in this point they weaken the agape motif. It is Paul that has the deeper insight into the meaning of agape. Yet as he admits, Paul also speaks of our agape for God, but not very often. By insisting that agape is independent of any influence from its object, does Nygren not fail to do justice to Christ's agape, which is characterized in the Gospels as being compassion stimulated by its objects? Since eros is part and parcel with human vitality, we cannot confine its association with agape to the conjugal love in marriage. But for Nygren agape can occupy no uncertain position between unmotivated and motivated love, and since the Johannine idea of agape does precisely this he feels it presents a peril within the Bible itself to the nature and content of agape.[9] Yet redemption does not bypass the human, but rather redeems it. Agape, therefore, is expressed within the sensitivity of human passion.

We find this compassionate sensitivity also in Paul. Writing to the Galatian congregation about whose welfare he is concerned, he describes his identification with them as the pains of a woman in labor with her child. "My little children, with whom I am again in travail until Christ be formed in you" (Gal. 4:19). He directs his readers to this same empathy. "Remember those who are in prison, as though in prison *with* them; and those who are ill-treated, since you *also* are *in the body*" (Heb. 13: 3, italics added). When this empathy is expressed through intercessory prayer, the priesthood of the believer is exercised according to its more catholic interpretation—namely, a priestly intercession patterned after the continuous high priestly intercession of Christ, who "is able for all time to save those who draw near to God through him, since he always lives to make intercession for them" (Heb. 7:25). The more Protestant conception of the priesthood of the believer stresses the accountability and responsibility of the individual. Consequently, Protestants find it difficult to *do* anything for others religiously.

While attending a pastoral conference on grief that included Roman Catholic and Protestant clergymen, I became aware that grief is a more difficult experience for the Protestant because he can do nothing for the deceased. Guilt is an aggravant in grief. We wish we could undo certain aspects of the past—relive them. Guilt demands its atonement. Remorse follows because it is too late to atone. Death is final, and after this there is only the judgment. But not so when you have purgatory. The bereaved Catholic can do something for the deceased— he can have masses said for him as often as he and the deceased have need.

Protestant individualism needs to be balanced by the responsibility of the believer, not only for his own state before God but for his priestly intercession regarding the needs of others with whom he is in some relationship of obligation—be he parent, child, neighbor, or friend. Intercession becomes genuine when the intercessor identifies himself in empathy with those for whom he intercedes. His intercession for others is his love for others directed heavenward.

The concern that manifests itself in intercessory prayer prepares the way for meaningful relationships between people. It is through such dialogues in depth that the concern of God is known. Consequently, knowing God not only helps us to know people, but knowing people helps us to know God. The relationship of rapport is the highway by which the Spirit of God communicates his Word. The priesthood of the believer is communicated to others by the empathy of the believer with the needs of others. As Christ is not someone apart from his people but is united with them, as the head among the members of the body, so we are members one of another in the same body. And when the foot hurts, the whole body feels it.

Although the knowledge of God is oriented to the believer's fellowship with God, it is a fellowship inseparable from the fellowship with the people of God. He is "Our Father." The intangible nature of God's fellowship is deepened in meaningfulness as well as safeguarded from human subjectivity by the more tangible nature of human fellowship. Paul's prayer in Ephesians for the "power to comprehend . . . what is the breadth and length and height and depth and to know the love of Christ which surpasses knowledge," is not expressed in isolation, but "with all the saints" (Eph. 3:18). Without the communion of saints, communion with God could generate into a monologue with oneself—into an unwholesome individualism if not egotism in which one begins to think of *himself* as the prime object of God's love. It is the resurgence of the infantile desire to be the "onliest child" rather than one of a family of children. Whoever confesses his faith in God also confesses his faith in the communion of saints, for he who loves God loves his brother also and whatever we do to the least of his brethren we do to him.

IV.
Knowing
and
Worship

The role that knowing God plays in our sanctification is indicative of the role that worship plays in sanctification, for knowing God is inseparable from the worship of God. When man is confronted by God, there is that unique response to which Rudolph Otto gave the name *numinous*—the subjective awareness of the presence of the Deity. If the awareness provokes terror, we flee like Adam to hide in the bushes. When the numinous is the response to God's overture of love, it is expressed as worship.

The various worship patterns that characterize the different bodies in Christendom show the difference in our interpretation of *knowing*. The Roman Catholic concern for the Eucharist reveals a conception of God objectivized in priestly cultus. The *numen* is present but there is also a gulf. Because of this, the *numinous* has the perspective of *aweful* respect. On the other hand, the orthodox Protestant concern for preaching stems from a conception of the Word of God as doctrine. God is objectivized, but more as an idea than a presence. Worship tends to merge with religious education. While the Roman Catholic churches followed the pattern of the temple worship, the Protestant churches took on the character of the synagogue.

The Wesleyan concentration upon religious warmth emphasizes God as feeling and inspiration rather than education as the means of knowing. While the Wesleyan recognition of the means of grace retains objectivity in worship, the trend is toward a subjectivized God. He is more immanent than transcendent, and the numinous is more the joy of intimacy than the awe and wonder of mystery. A more thoroughgoing subjectivization of God developed from the Anabaptist movement with its stress upon the *God-within*. A further subjectivism exists within the Society of Friends where the Sacraments are spiritualized and the Word of God is identified with the Inner Light. Here God is associated primarily with insight—the light within.

Each of these groups in Christendom has its own distinctive prayer pattern. Where God is objectivized as the transcendent presence the prayer abounds in the *numinous* quality. The presence is too much for mortal man. Under the old covenant even God's name—Yahweh—was too holy even to mention. The believer was confined to a human approximate of the name—Jehovah. When the concept of God is of such a transcendent nature, a priestly cultus of intermediaries and sacraments is a logical consequence. In Protestantism the emphasis on the *Word* leads to prayer as bold petition to God to act in the affairs of men. This is basic to Protestantism's concern for social reform—and the subsequent tendency to identify the reformed society with the kingdom of God. Among the more mystical, prayer tends to concentrate upon one petition, thy will be done, as an expression of becoming one with God. This mystical emphasis upon union with God rather than fellowship with God tends to blur the distinction between God and man. The contrast, says Brunner, is between "being alone and living for oneself" and "being with another and living for him."[10]

It is unfortunate that our divisions have separated rather than supplemented. Instead of recognizing what others are receiving from their traditions, our pride has moved us to exalt our own particular concept to the level of the ultimate. Confined to a monologue with our own group, we have accumulated all of the distortions of imbreeding. The initiation of dialogue that is taking place today within the divisions of Christendom has been urgently needed. Our vices lie in our self-acknowledged virtues. In isolation, Roman Catholic bodies tend to become superstitious. In orthodox Protestantism faith degenerates from knowing God to knowing the right doctrines about God. In the inspiration-centered groups, the multitude of holiness and revivalist descendants of the Wesleyan movement, there is the danger of equating religious with emotional. Those whose emphasis is on inward contemplation may be confusing God with the mysticism inherent in human nature. Those whose passion is for social justice may lose sight of the judgment upon all human society.

In our divisions we are in danger of identifying our distinctive worship formulas with knowing God. Then it is the formulas that are known rather than God. In worship one is confronted by the mystery of God. When worship patterns are the equivalent of worship the "witness of the Spirit" may be lost. What, then, is the effect on sanctification? When the fountainhead is affected, the waters cannot escape corruption. When God cannot be recognized beyond our patterns of worship, liturgical or non-liturgical, we are like Kierkegaard's drunken peasant who could not recognize his own legs because he had on a new pair of pants. How, then, can we be said to know him? The discrepancy is similar when we fail to recognize the Gospel in terminology other than our traditional words.

When worship is primarily performance, the sanctification which grows out of worship may also be performance. The elimination of the unstructured encounter leaves the door open for a culturally conditioned role for sanctification. The repeated failure of the church to rise above the shortcomings of its culture may be the result of such role-playing. When a member of the body begins to think of his own peculiar function as a principal if not the sole function of the body, he ceases to understand the nature of the body. How, then, can he know the Head?

According to the early church father Irenaeus, man is wholly man when his body and soul are united with the Spirit of God. Before his fall into sin Adam possessed this humanity as a child. Growth in this humanity was still before him. When he fell into sin, the creative process of God went awry. As the Redeemer of creation, Christ repeated the life of Adam in order to reverse the outcome from defeat to victory. Now the believer in Christ can carry on this restored humanity to maturity. By overcoming the barriers that had alienated us from the Spirit, Christ restored us to fellowship with the Spirit. Rather than being a supernatural addition to the human, the Spirit completes the human. Christ's victory over sin and death is the conquest of the natural over the unnatural.

But restoration to the fellowship with the Spirit means restoration also to the fellowship with our neighbor. As the believer continues to engage in the conflict with the devil that Christ has already fought and won for him, he gives expression to his restored humanity by loving his neighbor. Therefore, the fellowship of believers is the inevitable outcome of Christ's recapitulation of the life of Adam. The similarity of this teaching to the words of the prophet Micah illustrates Irenaeus' contention that the God of the Old Testament is the same as the God of the New Testament. "What does the Lord require of you, but to do justice, and to love kindness, and to walk humbly with your God" (Mic. 6:8).

Footnotes

1. Emil Brunner, *The Divine-Human Encounter* (Philadelphia: West-minster Press, 1943), p. 88.
2. See Dodd, *The Apostolic Preaching and Its Development*, pp. 17 ff. for the development of this primitive kerygma in the New Testament.
3. J. A. T. Robinson, *Honest to God* (London: SCM Press Ltd., 1963), p. 20.
4. Quoted in Rupp, *Righteousness of God*, p. 122. For original see *Luther's Works*, Vol. 34, p. 337.
5. Carroll Wise, *Pastoral Counseling* (New York: Harper & Row, 1951), p. 117
6. R. C. Zaehner, *At Sundry Times* (London: Faber & Faber, 1958), pp. 103, 181, 184.
7. Calvin, *Institutes* (Philadelphia: Presbyterian Board of Publication and Sabbath School Work), Vol. I, p. 4.
8. Luther, *The Freedom of the Christian Man* (Philadelphia: Fortress Press, 1947), p. 37 (pamphlet). For more recent translation, see *Luther's Works*, Vol. 31.
9. Anders Nygren, *Agape and Eros* (London: S.P.C.K., 1957), pp. 141, 150, 153, 222.
10. Brunner, *Divine-Human Encounter*, p. 153.

CHAPTER EIGHT

Maturity Through Dependence

The goal of sanctification is *teliotes,* which the King James Version of the Bible translates as *perfection,* and the Revised Standard Version and the New English Bible as *maturity.* The measure for this maturity is Christ himself. According to Ephesians the whole machinery of the church—apostles, prophets, evangelists, pastors, teachers—is for the "equipment of the saints," until we all attain to "mature manhood, to the measure of the stature of the fullness of Christ" (4:11-15). Rather than being children tossed to and fro—unstable and susceptible to the will of others—the Christian is to "grow up in every way into him who is the head, into Christ" (4:15). Says the writer to the Hebrews, "Therefore let us leave the elementary doctrines of Christ and go on to maturity" (6:1). The great Swedish pastor Schartau describes this maturity in Christ as a growth process in which "That which once and for all and immediately is reckoned as yours in justification will be worked in you little by little in sanctification."[1]

Is this maturity of sanctification the same maturity to which psychologists refer? Both, of course, refer to "growing up." But in sanctification the "growing up" is "into Christ." This is a process of maturing that is inseparable from the dynamic of *knowing* Christ. The dependency inherent in such *knowing* has all the earmarks of immaturity. Do religion and "mature manhood" really go together? Or did Freud have a point when he said that religion was a sign of immaturity—nothing but a projection of the father image into the universe? Instead of God creating man in his own image, man created God according to the image of his own needs because he was too dependent to face life as an adult without some continuation of the parent-child relationship. Religion is therefore an illusion—a neurotic symptom.

**I.
Religion
for the
Weak?**

Freud put into psychological terms what many believe to be true even though they know little of psychological theories. The physically strong self-made male may think that religion is fine for women and children, but for him it is simply a bore because he has no need for it. In church after church in this and other countries the women outnumber the men at worship far more than they do in the general population.

Behind this widespread belief that religion is for the weak is the tendency to think of God as another person. Normally we mature out of parental dependencies as we grow into adulthood. If we fail to mature we transfer this same dependency to a super-being whom we call God. Unfortunately there is some truth to Freud's position, for religion can easily degenerate into what he said it was. As a pastoral counselor to college students I spent much of my time helping young people extricate God—or what was left of him—from the projected mental image of their own parents.

Despite our mental images of him, God is not one being among others—even the Biggest Being. He is Being itself.

This is the understanding of God behind Tillich's ambiguous statement that God does not exist. Kierkegaard and before him Pseudo Dionysius said the same thing when they insisted that God is beyond existence. He is not one who exists, but he is the ground of existence. Consequently he cannot be described by adjectives as they apply to finite beings. God is infinite goodness, infinite wisdom. By the same token we cannot say that God loves, for others love also. Rather God *is* love. He is not *a* Spirit, but Spirit. So we must go to the "God beyond God" if we would know him—the God beyond that mental image of him into which we would shrink him.

The idea that religion is for the immature stems also from the error of thinking of God as someone external to us, as though he occupied a limited area of space as we do. God is Spirit. His Spirit bears witness with our spirits through the inner door of consciousness. This is why the Holy Spirit is difficult to objectify—to picture, compared with the ease with which we can picture the Father and the Son. His function places him too close to us. In his witness with our spirit, objectivity and subjectivity have no distinct borderline. Although God remains God and man remains man, the witness of the Spirit upon our spirits creates a relationship with God that allows for no psychological analysis or even dissection. Union with God is union with the Ground of Being in the depths of our own being.

Not only is maturity compatible with dependency upon God, but dependency upon God actually leads to maturity. This is the import of Jesus' answer to his disciples when they were in conflict over which of them was the greatest. Calling to him a child, Jesus placed him in the midst of them saying, "Whoever humbles himself like this child, he is the greatest in the kingdom of heaven" (Matt. 18:4). Does not this seem to contradict the purpose of growing up? Since the humility of a child is inseparable from his littleness and dependency, would this example not perpetuate childlike dependence? The mind of a child is an immature mind in contrast to the mind of a mature adult. Jesus seems to advocate a childlike dependency that as adults we desire to grow out of rather than into. That maturity should come with dependence rather than independence is in reverse direction from what we normally anticipate.

Is religion really for the weak? Actually it is for those who recognize their dependency. Superficially this may seem to be the same thing. When one lacks the human graces and strengths—when he is weak—it is difficult for him to believe in his own sufficiency. Conversely, when he has these graces and strengths—when he is strong—he has a natural tendency to take his sufficiency for granted. Yet, the fact remains that the weak may believe in their own sufficiency and the strong may recognize their dependency. More accurately, then, self-sufficiency goes with the irreligious and the recognition of dependency with the religious. Jesus' words, "Without me ye can do nothing," imply a thoroughgoing, existential dependency.

II.
Faith
to
Face

Despite the fact that our awareness of dependency prepares the way for faith in God, faith in God does not relieve us from facing the full force of the human predicament. Rollo May may disturb us when he says:

> The neurotic uses of religion have one thing in common: they are devices by which the individual avoids having to face his loneliness and anxiety. . . . But if the need to escape terror and loneliness are the main motives for turning to God, one's religion will not help him toward maturity or strength; and it will not even give him security in the long run. . . . Maturity and

eventual overcoming of loneliness are possible only as
one courageously accepts his aloneness to begin with.[2]

Is it really neurotic to use religion as an escape from
loneliness? May's point is that religion can be used to
avoid reality as well as to cope with it. Faith in God,
which is a personal relationship with God, is always in
tension with doubt, which is a personal *disrelationship*
with God. In the state of doubt we are painfully aware
of our isolation and the anxiety this realization provokes.
If our religion leads us to repress this awareness rather
than to face it, we are using it neurotically. When we
realize how often within religious circles doubt is viewed
as something shameful and its presence as a sign of dis-
loyalty to God, we are forced to take May's indictment
seriously. The strong faith is not the faith that knows no
doubt—this is the "scared" faith that survives by fleeing.
The strong faith is the faith that has known the full on-
slaught of doubt and has not only survived but has been
strengthened because of it.

I recall listening to a group of students giving their
testimony to passersby on the street before St. Aldate's
Church in Oxford. A statement by one of these young
men still remains in my mind. "There are 'bags of proof,'"
he said, "that God exists." So far as faith is concerned the
statement is surely so. But as a human being looking at
things from a human point of view, are there not also
"bags of proof" that God is an illusion? Or at best that he
and the devil groped out the world together, to use the
words of Robert Frost.[3] This is the problem in a day when
we are no longer receptive to the metaphysical arguments
for the existence of God, and the comfort they have
brought in the past. Instead of seeing the harmony in the
universe, we see the disharmony. This is the contemporary

human predicament, the agony of the existentialists, described by John Osborne as "the torture of being a human being"—the despair that emerges from the anxiety of emptiness and meaninglessness which dominates our age.

Yet it is not uniquely contemporary. In being tempted in all points as we are, Christ endured the agony of emotional isolation. He too knew what it meant to be alone, forsaken, empty. On the evening preceding his crucifixion the agony of the experience reached the intensity of bodily symptoms. "His sweat became like great drops of blood falling down upon the ground" (Luke 22:44). So fully did he enter into the despair and agony of one cut off from God that in his crucifixion he experienced that estrangement as his own. "My God, my God, why hast thou forsaken me?" These words seem strangely incongruous for the Messiah. Yet as the Archbishop of Canterbury has pointed out, "He is never more man's brother and never more 'totus in nostris' (wholly in us) than in the cry of dereliction."[4]

But this experience of being alone and forsaken is not a purely negative experience. Before one really discovers his potential, he may have to descend into the depths of defeat. Out of this confrontation with non-being he may achieve a very realistic faith in God. Yet this confrontation may also lead to a life without faith in God. Both affirmations call for a leap in faith and both require courage. Does it take more courage to be an Albert Camus or a Jean-Paul Sartre than a C. S. Lewis? Does it take more courage to leap confidently into darkness than into the arms of God?

While the question is open so far as courage is concerned, only one of the leaps requires the humility of submission. This is the difference between greatness in the world and greatness in the "kingdom of heaven." Affirmation of belief requires the humility of the child in its awareness of dependency. It requires the submission inherent in the relationship of the creature to the Creator. The alternative requires an affirmation of independence. The existentialist who affirms himself in a world of nothing may think it degrading to human dignity and insulting to human intelligence to surrender himself to a "God" differentiated from man. This declaration of independence on the part of the creature may not be far from creaturely defiance.

Obviously some experience must occur to move one to affirm himself in the midst of his despair. As described by an existentialist, this experience is devoid of sentiment whether it includes God or not. The existentialist position has the touch of stoic fortitude and discipline about it. Giving pre-eminence to the nakedness of faith and to the act of the will, it is predisposed to place its emphasis on courage in a heroic sort of self-affirmation. Of a different emphasis is the traditional description of the Christian response to Christ as typified in 1 Peter: "Without having seen him you love him; though you do not now see him you believe in him and rejoice with unutterable and exalted joy" (1 Peter 1:8). Here is a response in *feeling* to the revelation of God as *agape* whose warmth breaks in upon us. Although God breaks in upon us from without, it is difficult to extract this experience from the *believer's* existential moment. As Künkel describes the experience in one of his characters, "when he went down and hit the rock bottom of life he found love."[5] The leap in faith is a response to this disclosure of love.

Why does this disclosure occur to some—like C. S. Lewis —and not to others—like Bertrand Russell? This question takes us to the perennial tension between predestination and free will. Perhaps Brunner comes as close as anyone to resolving the enigma when he says, "To be gripped is at the same time to grip."[6] From a Christian point of view the reason why some have not received the disclosure of divine love is their defiance of dependency. It is an escape from the commitment of submission. In the last sermon that he preached at Oxford, John Baillie said, "God is He who is found by those who know that they themselves are lost. God is the name for the reality that breaks in upon our consciousness when we have surrendered our pride."[7]

In spite of the compelling nature of the divine overture the fact remains that as a member of the human race facing the human problem as a human being, the Christian is an agnostic. Otherwise his affirmation of belief is not a faith. The immature demand to see, to step carefully rather than leap, to know before they believe. If they are religious, they simply repress contradictory evidence. If they are irreligious, they demand proof. But the existential situation remains: there must be a leap. It is a leap over the *no* in life in the direction of the *yes*, even though that *yes* be the everlasting arms of love. Faith in God is an exercise in courage, and courage goes with maturity.

III.
Faith
or
Superstition

Our awareness of dependency is inseparable from our desire to pray. The simplest prayer is the plea of Simon Peter as he was sinking into the stormy sea, "Lord, save me!" The more inadequate and frightened a person feels, the more he calls upon God for help. Prayer then is something he does to get out of a "tight fix." It is a *cure*. But it also may develop into something that he does to keep from getting into the "fix." Then it is the *prevention*. Should he forget to offer this prevenient prayer, he may consider it the cause of unexpected mishaps. How far, then, is prayer removed from any other superstitious ritual? May the same weakness of personality that predisposes us to superstition predispose us also to religion—

in which case religion is simply a more refined and developed form of superstition? Too often we find our religion degenerating to this level of superstition, where, to get God to act on our behalf, we perform the prescribed ritual which presumably "does the trick." There is a subtle mingling of the superstitious with the religious in our personal or ecclesiastical rituals.

In spite of this affinity of religion with superstition, there remains a distinct contrast between superstition and faith—between magic and prayer. The magical incantations of superstition are attempts to control the "powers above" so that they may act in one's behalf or on behalf of the cultic group he represents. At least he tries to influence these powers not to interfere negatively with his affairs. This is the most crude form of *instrumentalism* in religion. Recognizing our dependency on the one hand and the powers that govern the universe on the other, we attempt to use those powers for our own purposes or at least to placate them for our own safety. Although such use of the Deity as an instrument for our own aggrandizement has its origin in our awareness of our dependency, it is actually a disguised attempt to affirm our *independence*. We seek control.

In the prayer of faith one puts himself in a position to *be* directed rather than to direct. God is allowed to remain the God-beyond-God, the unpossessed and uncoerced. Not that prayers of petition are low on the scale of Christian prayer. In fact the believer is encouraged to petition more. "You do not have, because you do not ask" (James 4:2). "Ask and you will receive" (John 16:24). However, we are not dependent on our own predisposition of how God should act in order to know that he is acting on our behalf. John Wesley brings in the distinctly Christian note of acceptance—something other than resignation—when he says, "The readiest way to escape from our sufferings is to *will* that they should continue so long as God proposes." This acceptance is the result of committing our petitions to God and receiving whatever transpires in terms of faith. This does not mean that God is the author of suffering or that he even wills it, but it does mean that he may accept such evils and utilize them for redemptive purposes. Having offered his petitions to God within the intimacy of his fellowship with God, the believer accepts the challenge of the proverb: "Trust in the Lord with all your heart, and do not rely on your own insight. In all your ways acknowledge him, and he will make straight your paths" (Prov. 3:5-6). Work thy ways, O Lord! We have moved from the self-centeredness that characterizes magic and superstition to the dedication and devotion that characterize prayer and faith.

In a previous chapter we referred to the man whose world had collapsed because a sudden illness had thwarted his vocational goals. His prayer life had ceased also because subconsciously at least he felt God had let him down. Up to that time God had been the One upon whom he had counted to help him accomplish his ambitions. Since his ambition was now frustrated, he could no longer relate to God on the old basis. During the transition that followed he was conscious religiously only of confusion. The magical aspect of his prayer life had come to a disappointing end, and there was nothing to replace it.

God may at times "withdraw" his presence so that he may reveal himself more fully. As he looked back over his experience the man said:

Man: It was rough—but as I said, I guess it had to be. I think I was exploiting God. He was just one more influential person I had "going" for me.

Pastor: You use the past tense.

Man: Yes—I hope it's past. I honestly think I have

grown in my faith. It is I who should be used by God rather than the other way around.

Pastor: Where before God was an instrument for gaining your ends, now you are the instrument for his ends.

Man: I'd like to think so. At least I hope it will be that way.

His new relationship to God is obviously on a more mature basis.

We have been using the term awareness of dependency without qualification. Actually a religious awareness of dependency is something different from a natural awareness. A natural awareness of dependency is simply a recognition of the obvious limitations of the finite and the mortal, and may lead to magical means for controlling the existing powers for our own defense. On the other hand, a religious awareness of dependency is an awareness of the *unobvious*. It is a recognition of weakness in strength, of inadequacy in the adequate, of evil in the good, of sin in man's higher nature. Consequently, a religious awareness of dependency comes not so much from natural observation as from the Spirit's witness to our spirits.

IV. Religious Dependency

Since it perceives inadequacy even in the adequate, religious awareness is awareness without ceasing. For how else can one be aware that his knowledge may be ignorance? In his *Enchiridion* Augustine says, "For although error ought to be avoided with all the care we can, not only in greater but also in lesser subjects, and although error is impossible except through ignorance of facts, yet it does not follow that one errs just because one is ignorant of something, but because one thinks one knows what one does not know." Augustine goes on to illustrate his point with an experience from his own life. On a certain journey he chose by mistake the wrong way at the crossroads, and by an indirect route he finally arrived at his destination. He discovered later that had he selected the right road, he would have been ambushed by a band of Donatists lying in wait for him. Commenting on this narrow escape Augustine said, "Hearing of those men's ambush I thought myself happy to have gone wrong, and for it gave thanks to God."[8]

Like Augustine some of us can look back upon certain life situations and in a hindsight marvel at God's guidance. And like Augustine at the actual time of the guidance we resisted any recognition of it because it did not fit the plan we had devised for that moment. How then can we transfer the faith evoked by hindsight to the actual moment when guidance is operative? Perhaps it is enough that we are permitted to see in retrospect how marvelously he works his ways. Perhaps it is part of our dependency that he should be guiding our ways when we are least aware of it.

The unceasing nature of a religious awareness of dependency is the basis for prayer without ceasing (1 Thess. 5:17). The one leads to the other. Based on the awareness of our potential inadequacy to measure up to any and every situation, the religious awareness of dependency is an existential dependency. Prayer without ceasing is simply a *conscious* dependency upon God, which in turn means a constant openness to receive. Should we become careless in our awareness of inadequacy, we open the door to the fall. When there is no awareness of dependency in any situation, there is no precaution, no "watch and pray that you may not enter into temptation." One can scarcely lose his awareness of dependence without falling into a spurious independence, as self-trust usurps trust in God, and loyalty to self replaces loyalty to God.

We in the church are constantly threatened by the outstanding people who are exceptions to this awareness of dependency. While Albert Schweitzer was a religious man, his fellow countryman and blood relative, Jean-Paul Sartre, is not. Schweitzer, of course, was an outstanding example of sacrificial service. Yet Sartre declined $50,000 and the honor of the Nobel Prize for Literature because of his convictions. He felt obligated, he said, to live out the principles for which he stands. Although no outward act can establish any particular inward motivation, we cannot help being impressed by both Schweitzer and Sartre.

Yet for Sartre these principles are of his own design. He believes that he and all others are their own creators. There is no meaning outside of himself for him to detect—rather he invents his own. Consequently, no matter how noble his convictions, he can change them at any time because he is his own authority. So it is difficult to see how he can take his obligations to himself with any great deal of seriousness. Yet he apparently does. But how many others could? With what do Sartre and others like him counteract the normal human tendency to selfishness?

Jesus' counsel to watch and pray is based on the reality of total dependence. Conversely it is based upon a total distrust in the human ability to withstand temptation in any and every circumstance. No day is easy to live. The very anticipation of ease makes us less aware of the unpredictable nature of each day, and as a result less aware of our own inadequacy to respond to the unpredictable. In addition, the anticipation of ease predisposes us to irritation at even minor disruptions of this ease. Consequently the day that promises to be easy to live may be the day of greater temptation. Describing this religious awareness of dependency as a "godly fear," Luther deemed it a necessary element in Christian living, since without it "the nerve of faith is out," and the Christian falls into the "evil ways of security" which is the "mother of hypocrites," or into despair.[9]

Besides coming from the world about us, other traditional sources of temptation are our own flesh and the devil. The devil was a reality in the thinking of the church from its beginning, through the Reformation, and until recent times. Bernard of Clairvaux instructed his monks in the art of withstanding temptation not only with reference to the reality of the devil, but even of demons. In our day the devil is depersonalized in psychological terminology. Yet it is quite possible that we are even less able to deal with temptation than the primitive animists who personalized every evil. Schiller raised the same question when he wrote:

> Like the dead striking of the pendulum-clock
> Nature, deprived of Gods,
> Slavishly serves the law of gravity.[10]

In the temptation stories of the Bible, evil is personalized. Satan's role in the fall of man is portrayed by the serpent who talks. In the story of Job he accuses Job before God. In Jesus' forty days of temptation in the wilderness, Satan even quotes Scripture. The words, "Get thee behind me, Satan," have been the means for resisting temptation down through the ages. The old division of the devil, the world, and our own flesh still has some value, and the petition "Lead us not into temptation" points to God as our deliverer from all three. Revealing this same dependence is the ancient morning collect:

> Grant us, O Lord, to pass this day in gladness and peace, without stumbling and without stain, that reaching the eventide victorious over all temptation through

thy ever present aid, we may praise thee, the eternal God, who dost govern all things and art blessed for evermore; through Jesus Christ, thy Son, our Lord.

SBH, p. 229, No. 80

So far as sanctification is concerned, it is the mark of wisdom to have a wholesome respect for one's adversaries.

This dependency upon God is inseparable from our fellowship with God. Although fellowship goes far beyond the primitive "Lord, save me!" it is never dissociated from it. To live at the demanding edge of life is to live where we are continually reminded of our dependency. If we seek instead the safety and security of inactivity and withdrawal, dependency is obviously offensive. Faith in God is an adventure with God, and is exercised by the existential awareness of dependency in the adventure. Fellowship is dynamic in adventure and static in the security of self-limitation.

What we can endure and what we think we can endure may be two different things. If we do not expose ourselves to situations that would demand more from us than we think we can master, we give God little chance to develop our potential. Yet, there is the necessary tension over whether we are the victims of our own arbitrary self-limitations or whether we are wisely recognizing our obvious limitations. The times when we are literally forced by unplanned circumstances into situations we would normally think beyond our capacity to endure may bring to light potentials that otherwise we would block. Our problem is that we pray for spiritual growth, but are hesitant to assume the conditions that might stimulate such growth. Therefore we may question whether we really want to grow. Jesus' question to the paralytic by the pool of Bethesda—"Do you *want* to be healed?" (John 5:6)—was revealing because the man was supposedly at the pool for this purpose.

**V.
Independence
Through
Dependence**

A religious awareness of dependence leads to independence from other dependencies. Total independence for the human being is an illusion. "Man is most free," says Niebuhr, "in the discovery that he is not free."[11] When one affirms his independence from God, he is led into other dependencies that can "sift us as wheat." The atonement of Christ that reconciles us to God is the victory of God over the enslaving tyrants of the human being—sin, death, devil, law, guilt, fear, hate. Enslavement to these tyrants causes the self to center on itself—a condition that leads inevitably to disintegration. The atonement breaks the power of the tyranny and releases the self so it can center on God, the only real alternative.

Through the victory of Christ, our very dependence upon God integrates us in the depths of our being so that we can withstand the onslaughts of the external forces associated with the problem of evil. The agape that liberates us is also the agape that unites us. Through the atonement we establish a dependence upon the source of Being so that we may remain independent of the forces of non-being that threaten to possess us. "For freedom Christ has set us free" (Gal. 5:1). Here is a dependence that strengthens us to cope positively with reality, and this is what we mean by maturity. "Apart from me you can do nothing" (John 15:5) has its other side in, "I can do all things in him who strengthens me" (Phil. 4:13). "Aware of thine almightiness," writes Fenelon, "I am not afraid of my weakness."[12] Therefore, "when I am weak, then I am strong" (2 Cor. 12:10).

To progress in maturity means to progress in the intensification of dependency awareness. In this progress we not only go beyond the commonly understood dependencies of our own finitude and the limitations due to our misuse of freedom, but we also become increasingly aware of our susceptibility to the loss of faith in our perspective.

While this loss is a result of the fact that our self is curved in upon itself, it is in a different category from the other results of this curvature. It shows itself when we are reluctant to recognize God in any situation where we had not first planned to recognize him. In our attitudinal myopia we fail to recognize any reality beyond what we had anticipated, and so lose the opportunity to depend on God in the unstructured moment.

Because we become enslaved to our preconceived notions, self-limited experiences, and cultural thought patterns, our receptivity to revelation is exceedingly dim. Because of our set ways of looking at things, it may not even occur to us that our viewpoint could be wrong or at least only a partial viewpoint and that God's view may be quite different. When we realize that God respects human freedom we know what barriers we erect by our closed minds. Every present moment has eternal significance because God has redeemed it through Christ. The person who leaves room in his attitudes for the larger vision and will of God will experience life as an adventure with God. Even in the doldrums of the daily routine he will not only see *things* but will see God in, through, and beyond the things.

Literacy missionary Frank Laubach relates two insights from his own experience concerning the relationship between maturity and the expansion of our dependency awareness. Most of us feel some degree of inadequacy before we make a speech and may pray for help. But this prayer is still on the primitive level of awareness. As he grew in his understanding of religious dependency, Laubach realized that it was not only he who needed help to communicate, but also his hearers needed help to be open for his communication. As he enlarged his intercession to include them, his concern for the occasion rose above the usual egocentric fears.

On another occasion he was bogged down with a back-log of work and wished not to be disturbed. When the phone rang he was irritated, and his primary concern was to return to his work. As he answered the phone, the thought occurred to him that it was just such a closed frame of mind that had caused him to be oblivious in the past to obvious realities, and he directed this recol-lection to God with the petition that he might be open to divine guidance. What happened made a lasting im-pression. Because of his awareness he "had ears to hear" what normally he would not have heard. As a conse-quence, what most surely would have been only a per-functory interruption in an already harried day became a very meaningful moment for a troubled caller.

To be open to receive is a functional definition of what it means to have faith in God. It is also what we mean by an existential awareness of our dependency. For this reason the person who is achieving maturity through his dependency does not claim maturity for himself. In view-ing himself from the vantage point of dependency, he "has eyes to see" only too clearly what he yet lacks. Be-cause maturity develops out of dependence, it must of necessity develop along with humility. The freedom in-herent in the maturity of sanctification directs itself in devotion to the community. Luther's propositions in his *Treatise on Christian Liberty* express this paradoxical relationship between freedom and service. "A Christian man is a perfectly free lord of all, subject to none. A Chris-tian man is a perfectly dutiful servant of all, subject to all."[13]

VI. Dependency at Heart of Maturity

Since the direction of growth is from being centered in oneself to becoming devoted to God and through God to others, it is clear that in sanctification love and maturity go together. Agape has been described as one-way love, and in a sense it is. By its very nature agape does not depend for its existence upon its object. Because it is unconditional it does not have to be reciprocated. But this is only part of the story. Although agape is given without the necessity of a response, its purpose is not complete until there is a response. Since God is agape, we see the need for this completion in his desire for the response of faith from those whom he loves. In his covenant, God gives himself when he bestows his grace, but the covenant is not complete until man gives himself to God in his response in faith. "God's children are grateful and therefore are free," says Barth.[14] Those who desire only to give and not to receive are manifesting the pride of self-sufficiency rather than agape love. This association of giving with receiving is seen in the analogy of the body of Christ. The members of the body are united by agape, but this agape is experienced in mutual dependence. Even Christ as the Head shares in this dependence upon the rest of the body.

Is the Creator dependent upon the creature? One of the cardinal attributes of God is that he is dependent upon no one. He is in himself totally and unqualifiedly sufficient. The gist of God's reply to Job, for example, seems to be that he is answerable to no one. "Where were you when I laid the foundation of the earth?" (Job 38:4). "Can you lift up your voice to the clouds, that a flood of waters may cover you?" (38:34). Since the whole of God's reply is in this vein, the point seems to be that between the finite and the infinite there is a great gulf, and where the creature obviously is dependent upon the Creator, the dependency is not mutual.

But Archibald McLeish—who has become somewhat of an authority on the Book of Job at least dramatically through his *JB*—says no. The Book of Job, he says, reveals the dependency, not only of the creature upon the Creator, but also of the Creator upon the creature. He bases this argument on the theme of the book, "Does Job fear God for nought?" (1:9). This is the taunt that Satan throws in the face of God. Does Job's devotion to God go deeper than his own personal advantage?

God made man in his own image so that he might have a creature with whom he could fellowship. This fellowship is experienced when the creature responds to the love of his Creator. Faith reaches its maturity in the creature when he "fears God for nought." Then God's agape has completed its task. In a sense, therefore, God also participates in the universal dependency. He wants something from us. If desires indicate needs, then God needs our love. It is Eliphaz, the first comforter, not Job, who presents the doctrine of divine indifference. "Can a man be profitable to God? Surely he who is wise is profitable to himself. Is it any pleasure to the Almighty if you are righteous, or is it gain to him if you make your ways blameless?" (Job 22:2-3). But if God loves, cares, grieves, and joys over the one lost sheep, over the one sinner who repents, then he is anything but indifferent. "The concept of God without man," says Barth, "is indeed as anomalous as wooden iron."[15] The greater our sanctification, the more we fear God "for nought." Maturity is grounded in dependence and dependence reaches its maturity when it approaches agape—when it becomes a dependence not only for the believer's sake but also for God's sake. Francis Xavier has expressed it in verse.

My God, I love Thee—not because
    I hope for heaven thereby,
Nor yet because those who love Thee not
    Are lost eternally.

Not with the hope of gaining aught;
Not seeking a reward;
But as Thyself hast loved me,
O ever-loving Lord.

E'en so I love Thee, and will love.
And in Thy praise will sing;
Solely because Thou art my God,
And my eternal King.[16]

Footnotes

1. *Henric Schartau and the Order of Grace* (Rock Island: Augustana, 1928), p. 123.
2. Rollo May, *Man's Search for Himself* (New York: W. W. Norton & Co., 1953), pp. 202-203.
3. Robert Frost, *A Masque of Reason* (New York: Henry Holt & Co., 1945), p. 11.
4. A. M. Ramsey, *The Gospel and the Catholic Church* (London: Longmans, 1956), p. 23.
5. Fritz Künkel, *In Search of Maturity* (New York: C. Scribner's Sons, 1948), p. 216.
6. Brunner, *Divine-Human Encounter,* p. 151.
7. From a sermon preached by John Baillie in St. Mary the Virgin Church, Oxford, June, 1959.
8. St. Augustine, *Enchiridion* (London: S.P.C.K., 1953), pp. 14-15.
9. Rupp, *op. cit.,* p. 178.
10. From *The Gods of Greece,* quoted by Bultmann, *The Presence of Eternity* (New York: Harper, 1957), p. 101.
11. R. Niebuhr, *op. cit.,* I, 260.
12. *Meditations and Devotions of Fenelon, op. cit.,* p. 36.
13. Luther, *Treatise on Christian Liberty* (Philadelphia: Fortress Press, 1947), p. 5.
14. K. Barth, *The Holy Ghost and the Christian Life* (London: Frederick Muller, Ltd., 1938), p. 83.
15. K. Barth, *The Humanity of God* (Richmond: John Knox Press, 1960), p. 72.
16. *Congregational Praise* (London: Independent Press Ltd., 1951), p. 461.

CHAPTER NINE

Hope or Fulfillment

Ours is a "sanctification" rather than a "justification" age. We are more interested in progress than in forgiveness. Implying movement toward a goal, progress is reassuring to our anxiety over meaninglessness. In contrast, the period of the Reformation was a guilty age, and *justification* spoke to the need. Although oriented toward sanctification, we are less likely to experience it. If, as Tillich says, "nothing greater can happen to a person than that he is forgiven,"[1] those who prefer instead to see progress may end up only with an illusion of progress.

Sanctification is as elusive as the humility which characterizes it. Once humility is identified, it may cease to be humility. Like an eel it slips through our fingers in the very attempt to grasp it. Our attempts to be humble or even to describe humility are more open to caricature than to anything else. So great is this danger that one must continually ask himself if this is also what is happening to his understanding of sanctification.

Obviously this work has produced no last word on the subject. Because of our susceptibility to delusion and deception, the Word of God can become something other

178

after we have received it. By maintaining a balance between theological reflection and experiential insights, it
is my hope that we have avoided the major pitfalls. But
it remains a hope. In the area of sanctification it should
be obvious that no one has *the* answer. The humility that
is essential to sanctification is essential also to an understanding of sanctification. The same dependency that
undergirds our maturity must undergird our inquiry into
this maturity.

The need for progress is our cultural expression of the
ancient desire for perfection. With the evolutionary concept permeating all phases of the human enterprise, we
find it difficult to think in any other category. Life that
does not change, perishes. Industry, for example, has its
timetable for tangible results. Corporations that do not
keep abreast of the changing scene by thinking ahead and
branching out will lose out to the more progressive firms.
Perfectionists in the church have made their mark in the
history of sanctification. Bishop Neill sees them as gadflies
to sting the church into alertness when it is overcome with
the "placid acceptance of mediocrity."[2] But the trend to
perfectionism pertains to more than a creed or to a sec-
tarian movement. It involves the universal human desire
to "wrap things up"—to "have it made"—to be assured of
progress. Ours is a passion for completion.

I. The Passion for Perfection

The passion for perfection is actually a form of the
pleasure principle as set forth by Freud. When things are
going well and all is positive and satisfying, we flare up
at any intrusion of imperfection to mar our elation. On
the other hand, we can better adjust to imperfection when
we are dispirited, for we are already accustomed to disappointment. This acceptance of disappointment provides
us further insight into the sanctifying influence of the
crucifixion experience. By enabling us to accept more

readily the negative factors of existence, it prepares us for the resurrection of hope in the positive factors. Reconciliation with defeat rather than resignation prepares the way for deliverance. The recognition of defeat opens us to the influence of the Holy Spirit through whom we receive the renewed hope.

We see these tendencies in their extreme forms in manic-depressive psychosis. The manic stage corresponds to the perfectionist dream. At the sacrifice of reality, the manic is intensely elated about his life. Yet his very intensity is the symptom of his desperation. He is running from the negative, the imperfect, the depressing. Once these negative realities about himself catch up to him, he will swing to the other extreme and become intensely depressed. Now the imperfections of his life overwhelm him, and his outward appearance of spiritlessness hides the anguish and agitation that he cannot express. Truth lies in neither extreme, but in a paradoxical center where one can take in both the positive and the negative. The present tense is always characterized by the "dialectical between" in which desire and disappointment remain in tension with each other. The cross of Christ is God's rejection of all perfectionist schemes.

Life in this world is neither heaven nor hell; it is a fluctuating mixture of the two. The separation of good from evil is an eschatological hope. Since we have a penchant for absolutes in terms of blacks and whites, we are ill-fitted for our complicated existence in the grays. Perfection is an anticipation associated with "waiting upon the Lord." Our offense at postponing perfection is another example of our resistance to dependency. In spite of this resistance, our tension over the unfulfilled remains. The basis for godly contentment is not a simple acceptance of imperfection. This could be indifference or even cynicism. Godly contentment is based upon an acceptance of imperfection that is united with a vision of the perfect. This vision provides challenge as well as hope.

Perfectionism as a creed arises out of our common human need for absolutes. It is difficult to understand how a person with any insight into himself could possibly believe he had arrived at a state of perfection—especially in our day when popular psychology has exposed our rationalizations and repressions—regardless of how reduced his definition of perfection may be. Yet perfectionism as a creed satisfies some basic human needs. For one thing, it offers a decisive stand. Here is a definite statement about sanctification in contrast to the usual vague and ill-defined concepts. Even more important, it brings drama where drama has been sadly lacking. The "holiness" teaching that sanctification is the second act of grace takes to itself some of the romance of conversion. Now there is something beyond conversion to take the monotony out of Christian growth—something which dramatically completes conversion in the here and now. Regardless of our difficulty in describing it, the way of sanctification is never monotonous or undramatic. The dynamic of crucifixion and resurrection is a turbulent experience. The extension of redemption into the full scope of creation is a continuous challenge. The walk by faith is a venture in anticipation. The covenant relationship with the Spirit is a stimulus—however fluctuating—for identity and purpose.

Previously our romantic dramas climaxed in the marriage vows, as though life after marriage had little drama left. Today our more mature romantic drama extends into the actual experiences of married life. Our need also is to mature religiously. Not only the events leading to conversion and conversion itself are of dramatic interest, but events within the converted life. There is drama in the

Christian *life* and not just in the prelude. However, when our concept of sanctification degenerates into character traits, perfectionism provides a contrast in vitality.

But perfectionism as a creed is older than Wesley and the holiness groups. It is found in the early church and especially in Augustine. Says Barth in criticism of Augustine's perfectionist teachings, "It is only too plain [from] his [Augustine's] language [that] there is a spirit of fulfillment in place of the Spirit of Promise who is the Holy Ghost."[3] We see in the lust for perfection an offense to *hope* and a resistance to *promise*. We want it all here and now. Guilt, then, would be an evidence of failure. How, then, can it exert its constructive influence as a sorrow with hope? In remorse, guilt is destructive because one sorrows without hope. Among those who anticipate perfection, guilt is likely to be repressed because it contradicts the anticipation. Now there is no sorrow. They do not choose to "know in part," but want to "understand fully." The eschatological dimension of the Christian message is an offense to them.

Like the prophecies of the Old Testament, our insights into sanctification are not crystal clear. Those who prophesied, says Peter, searched and inquired into their revelation. So also our insights into sanctification are not "bull's eyes." They require us to search and inquire. Nevertheless, as with the Old Testament prophecies, these insights still communicate understanding. As an integral part of our dependency upon God, the eschatological dimension of sanctification is a counteractive to the lust for perfection. "It does not yet appear what we shall be, but we know that when he appears we shall be like him, for we shall see him as he is. And every one who thus hopes in him purifies himself as he is pure" (1 John 3:2-3). Hope is a dynamic thrust into the future as well as a dynamic pull from the future. As such it counteracts directly the anxiety that arises over threats inherent in the future. Hope has as strong an influence upon our *purification* as those other abiding gifts, faith and love.

Faith, hope, and love overlap each other so that definitions of one include references to the others. If these "fruit of the Spirit" belong to the whole person, they cannot be classified with specific phases of the person such as the Thomistic relegation of faith to an intellectual assent to dogma. Faith works through love, and apart from love it is dead. Yet faith as belief can be differentiated from love. Faith is inseparable from hope because it involves trust regarding the future. Yet faith as an existential commitment is differentiated from hope. But of the three it is love alone that belongs also to the eternal age. Thus its greater attraction to our lust for the perfect. Faith and hope belong to the realm of the incomplete. They permit us to penetrate the dark glass of our earthly existence, only to be superseded by the clarity of our eternal destiny. But that clarity is not yet. In the meantime, faith and hope are as necessary as love.

Is the only alternative to perfection a complacency with imperfection? Or is this alternative the false deduction from a point of view that is dependent upon the human need for completion? The middle term between perfection and imperfection for the Christian is gratitude. In a sense the Christian is becoming what he already is. The Christian life is a matter of desiring completion without having to have it. It is a matter of striving for something which we have already attained by *faith*, but which we have yet to work out by *sight*. It is a mark of growth to learn to live with imperfection without being satisfied with it—to be content with Christ's righteousness without ceasing to strive for our own.

From whatever dimension we approach sanctification, we find ourselves focusing on the person of Christ as the incarnation of God who is agape. Such has been the case whether we focused on the divine initiative or the human response—for the mystery of the incarnation embodies them both. As God, Christ brings God's grace to man, and as man he addresses himself to God. Thus he contains within himself the mutuality of the covenant relationship between God and man. This mutuality was evident at his Baptism when he submitted to this initiatory rite of the new covenant against the wishes of John, who recognized him as the inaugurator of the new covenant. "Let it be so now," Jesus said, "for thus it is fitting for us to fulfil all righteousness" (Matt. 3:15). He expresses in himself the covenant ties.

As we focus on the person of Christ in sanctification, we are dealing with the doctrine of the real presence. Although associated with the Lord's Supper, the real presence has a wider application as the *divine objectivity*. The real presence is the heavenly mystery that ties together all Christian doctrine. Doctrines are not simply religious truths—any more than the means of grace are simply holy things. The risen Christ gives to each its dynamic for sanctification. Functioning within the mystery of relationship, the real presence accounts for our inability to conceptualize this sanctification.

This concentration of everything in the real presence of the Incarnate One is essentially what Paul means when he says that he is determined "to know nothing among you except Jesus Christ and him crucified" (1 Cor. 2:2). In this affirmation Paul emphasizes the unity of the Word of God with the person and sacrifice of Christ. We find this same union of the Word with the person and the person with the sacrifice in the Synoptic Gospels and in the

Fourth Gospel. It is the person of Christ whom we know through his sacrifice. This is no distorted Christ-centeredness which neglects the Father and the Spirit. Rather it is the Pauline concentration upon Christ as the One whom the Father has sent and who in turn sends the Spirit. The God who was in Christ reconciling the world to himself is the Triune God.

Since it is the Lord's person that unites his word and his act, his influence upon us cannot be fully understood or even adequately described. It is veiled behind the mystery not only of personhood but of that which happens between persons—what Barth calls the "secret of the Holy Ghost." Here we must bow before the reality that we are looking through a glass darkly. These are the things of the Spirit which 2 Peter says are hard to understand—until the day dawns and the morning star rises in our hearts (3:16, 1:19). The Christian hope strengthens us for the great leap of faith. All other challenges to faith are shadows of the leap in the face of death and serve to exercise and condition us for this leap. The One whom we know is called *I Am*—the eternally present One. Our hope is that the relationship which we have with him can endure the threat of our own death because it participates in his eternal present. God said unto Moses, "I am the God of Abraham, and the God of Isaac, and the God of Jacob"—for "He is not God of the dead, but of the living" (Mark 12:26-27). The relationship once established is established forever. This is the eternal hope of the Christian message—the living hope of the Christian experience. When faith is fulfilled in understanding, and hope is replaced by completion, then the greatest of these, love, shall abide in perfection.

Footnotes

1. Paul Tillich, *The New Being* (New York: Scribners, 1955), p. 7.
2. Stephen Neill, *Christian Holiness* (New York: Harper & Row, 1960), p. 114.
3. Karl Barth, *The Holy Ghost and the Christian Life* (London: Frederick Muller, Ltd., 1938), p. 74.

Index

187